THE

Yorkshire Anglers' Guide

TO THE WHOLE OF THE

FISHING ON THE YORKSHIRE RIVERS.

TOM BRADLEY

OLICANA BOOKS
1979

First published Leeds 1894
Republished Olicana Books 1979

ISBN 0 903116 04 9 (Cloth)
ISBN 0 903116 05 7 (Leather)

Printed and bound in Great Britain by
The Scolar Press Ilkley West Yorkshire

THE

Yorkshire Anglers' Guide

TO THE WHOLE OF THE

FISHING ON THE YORKSHIRE RIVERS.

BY

TOM BRADLEY,

AUTHOR OF

The "Yorkshire Rivers," "The Old Coaching Days in Yorkshire," &c.

PRICE EIGHTEENPENCE.

Leeds:

TOM BRADLEY, 20, GREEN'S COURT, BRIGGATE.

1894.

PREFATORY NOTE.

THIS work originally formed a series of successful articles which appeared weekly, from April to November, 1892, in the columns of that high-class Angling Journal, *The Fishing Gazette.* Since that time, those articles have been carefully revised and corrected, and are now presented to the Angling Public in a collective form. As both private and club waters are subject to constant changes, the author will feel obliged to anyone pointing out any such changes or errors in the present work, in order that they may be rectified in future editions.

LEEDS, 1894.

YORKSHIRE ANGLERS' GUIDE.

RIVER AIRE.

The River Aire rises suddenly from the ground in a volume at Aire Head (620 feet above the sea), in the pastures below Kirkby Top, and about half-a-mile south of Malham. About 200 yards from its source it is joined by the Malham and Gordale Becks, which are really the main tributaries of the infant river, the former flowing through the village from Malham Tarn, the latter from Gordale Scar and the moors beyond. The Aire empties itself into the Ouse at Asselby Island below Airmyn, about two miles north-west of Goole, after running in a polluted condition through Leeds, Castleford, Knottingley, and Rawcliffe. From Bradford Beck to its mouth it is in a state of putrid corruption, and the portion of the river that concerns the angler lies above Baildon Bridge. The principal angling tributaries besides those mentioned are Otterburn Beck, Eshton Beck, Eller Beck, Cononley Beck, Eastburn Beck, Silsden Beck, River Worth (polluted), and Harden Beck. Some of these are first-class trout streams, but are in strictly private hands. The upper length of the River Aire is one of the best trout streams in Yorkshire, the best length being probably owned by the Aire Fishing Club. Malham (two inns) is five miles from Bell Busk, which is the nearest railway station, and eleven miles from Skipton.

The fishing from the source to Airton is in strictly private hands, but visitors to Malham are granted permission to fish Malham Beck from the Cove to the river, and Gordale Beck from the Scar to the main stream, each length of water being about a mile and a half. At Kirkby Malham three-quarters of a mile below Aire Head, there is an inn. Airton is two miles and a quarter from the source, and three miles from Bell Busk Station.

The Yorkshire Anglers' Association water extends on the right, or Airton, side of the river from Airton Bridge to the footbridge at Bell Busk Hills (one and three-quarter miles). President of the association, J. P. Hubbersty, M.A.; vice-presidents, J. D. Johnstone and Henry Cadman; council, Henry Bradshaw, Henry Cadman, Isaac Gaunt, John Gerrard, R. T. Hadow, M.A., Cyril Ransome, M.A., C. E. Moody, Walter Rowley, C.E., and F. M. Walbran; hon. secretary, T. E. Pritt, Lytonville, Headingley; river watcher, Simon Bell, Calton. Limited to one hundred members; elected by ballot; very exclusive. Annual subscription, £1 11s. 6d.; entrance fee, £1 1s. No short period tickets. Two friends allowed to fish in company with a member. The principal water of this association, however, is on the Eamont, where they have seven and a-half miles of first-class fishing near to Brougham Castle, and about one mile from Penrith. Close time on the Aire, October 2nd to March 16th; on the Eamont, October 16th to March 16th. Trout under 7in. to be returned. No clear water worm fishing before July 1st. No other restrictions on any kind of legitimate fishing. In the Eamont, both salmon and trout are first-class; in the Aire, nothing but trout, which run about three to the pound. Calton, where the watcher lives, is on the opposite bank to Airton. Tarn Dyke enters the river about a mile below Airton. This dyke runs from Eshton Tarn, which holds some large pike. Bell Busk Hills, where the Yorkshire Anglers' Association water ends, is a mile and three-quarters below Airton Bridge, and half-a-mile from Bell Busk Station. About half-a-mile below, on the right, Otterburn Beck enters. A good trout stream but private. The fishing from the opposite side to the Yorkshire Anglers' Association is private. The fishing from Bell Busk Hills to Gargrave (four miles) is private on both sides. About a mile above Gargrave the Leeds and Liverpool Canal crosses the river by an aqueduct. There is some fair pike fishing in the canal at this point, but permission is needed from the company.

The proprietors generally allow the villagers to fish the river where it runs through the village green of Gargrave from the High Green to the weir. This embraces about half-a-mile of nice water. At Gargrave there are several inns and a railway station. The Aire Fishing Club length commences at Gargrave, and extends to Eastburn Beck end. The water is divided into two sections, Section A extending from Gargrave to Carleton Stone Bridge, Section B from Carleton Stone Bridge to Eastburn Beck. Both sides of the river are entirely in the hands of the club, except a few fields between Kildwick Bridge and Eastburn, which are owned by the Bradford Eagle Angling Association. The Aire Club has been established since 1838. President, J. R. Tennant, Esq.; hon. secretary, T. H. Dewhurst, Esq., Skipton. Limited to twenty members for Section A, and fifty members for Section B. Annual subscription, £6 6s.; entrance fee, £5 5s. This covers both sections. Section B alone, 20/-. No short period tickets issued. Close time for trout, October 2nd to March 15th; for grayling, March 15th to June 15th. Trout under 8in. to be returned. The tributaries are strictly private. The fishing is of the very highest class. The river contains trout, grayling, chub, roach, perch, and pike. The club have a fish-breeding establishment, and turn an annual supply of young trout into the river The lengths of the club water following the course of the river are: Section A, four and three-quarter miles; Section B, a little over six miles. Total length about eleven miles. The places *en route* are Thorlby (inn), two and a-half miles below Gargrave. Carleton (inns), four miles. Skipton (several inns and railway station), five miles. Cononley (inn and railway station), eight and a quarter miles. Cross Hills (inns and railway station), nine and three-quarter miles; and Kildwick (inns), ten and a quarter miles. Eshton Beck enters about a mile below Gargrave, and Broughton Beck about a mile above Carleton; both are good private trout streams.

From Kildwick Bridge to Eastburn Beck, on the right side of the river, the Bradford Eagle Angling Association comes in. President, Mr. C. H. Thompson; hon. secretary, Mr. H. S. Foulds. Sixty members. Not limited. Entrance fee, 2s. 6d.; monthly subscription, 6d. The length of this water is about three-quarters of a mile. On the opposite side the fishing belongs to the Aire Club, as above mentioned.

At Eastburn Beck, the Stockbridge and Eastburn Angling Club commence. Their length extends to the River Worth, below Stockbridge, both sides without a break. President, Councillor W. A. Robinson ; vice-presidents, Messrs. J. Groves, R. H. Padget, W. H. Whitaker, William Naylor, and W. Harrison ; hon. secretary Mr. Ellis, Town, Keighley ; treasurer, Mr. Jos. Smith ; river watchers, R. Hill, Silsden, and T. Hardacre, Beatrice Street, Keighley. Membership unlimited ; at present, about one hundred. Annual subscription, 10s. ; youths under twenty-one, 5s. When ten days' tickets have been purchased the holder is entitled to a full member's ticket. Day tickets for outsiders, 1s., procurable from the secretary, river watchers, or at the Bridge Inn, Stockbridge ; Roebuck Inn, Utley ; Bridge Inn and Red Lion Inn, Silsden ; also from Messrs. R. H. Padget, ironmonger, Keighley ; Joseph Smith, Market Place, Keighley ; J. W. Mitchell, saddler, Ghurch Green, Keighley ; and John Wood, hairdresser, North Street, Keighley. Close time for trout, October 2nd to March 16th. Trout under 8in. to be returned. This length of water is well stocked with trout, perch, chub, roach, and gudgeon, with occasional pike, dace, grayling, and eel. For some years the club have turned an annual supply of Loch Leven trout into their water. Last year the number was 18,000, and the sport is improving yearly. Trout up to 3-lbs. weight have been caught. The water abounds in deeps, for the float-fisher and for fly-fishing the streams above and below Steeton Bridge and at Howden are the best. Howden feeder is the chief breeding beck. No Sunday fishing allowed.

From Eastburn Beck, at the commencement of the Stockbridge and Eastburn Angling Club water, to Stockbridge, where it ends, it is five and a quarter miles. The places *en route* are Steeton and Silsden, one and a quarter miles (railway station and inns). Utley, three and three-quarter miles (inns). Stockbridge and Utley are each one mile from Keighley, where there are numerous inns and a railway station. Howden is on the opposite side of the river to Utley.

The River Worth, which is polluted, enters just below Stockbridge. From this point to Bingley Bridge (three and a quarter miles), the fishing on the left, or Riddlesden, side, and from Stockbridge Weir to Marley Sandhills (one and three-quarter miles), on the right side, is in the hands of the tenants, from whom permission is easily obtained, except where the private grounds of Longwood and The Hills come in between Castlefields and Bingley. The fishing, however, between Stockbridge and Bingley is of little or no good, particularly in the top length, on account of the pollution which enters from the River Worth. At Marley Sandhills the Bradford Angling Association's water commences, and extends on the right side of the river to the Bingley end of Hollins Wood (one and a half miles) without a break. This club, which was formed in October, 1879, has about fifty members. The water previously belonged to the Bingley Angling Club, which is now defunct. The fishing is only poor.

At Bingley there are several inns and a railway station. From Bingley Bridge to Cottingley Bridge (one and a quarter miles) the fishing is private on both sides. About half-a-mile below Bingley Bridge, a private trout stream called Harden Beck enters the river. From Cottingley Bridge to Baildon Bridge (about three miles), the fishing on both sides belongs to the Saltaire Angling Association (formed 1867). President, Edward Salt, Esq.; chairman, Albert Swaine, Esq.; secretary, Mr. Henry Sayner, 25, Titus Street, Saltaire; river watcher, Willis Hall. Number of members, 100 (not limited). Annual subscription, 5s.; youths from fifteen to eighteen, 2s. 6d.; boys under fifteen, for whom parents or guardians will be responsible, 2s. 6d. Day tickets, 1s., procurable from the secretary; also from Messrs. J. Hall, Market Street, Bradford; A. F. Wilson, 5, Westgate, Shipley; Richard Holgate, Main Street, Bingley; and J. E. Parker, Saltaire. Trout under 8in. to be returned. All legal baits allowed. No Sunday fishing. No fishing between 11-0 p.m. and 3-0 a.m. One rod only. The coarse fishing is good. There is also some fair trout fishing in the top reaches.

Saltaire, where there is a railway station, is about three-quarters of a mile above the bottom limit. Shipley stands on the right side of Baildon Bridge. Several inns and railway station. On the Shipley side of the river, just below the bridge, the Bradford Beck enters, and the remainder of the river is in a state of rampant pollution. The total length of the fishable water on the Aire is thirty-two and a quarter miles. Total length of the river from the source to where it enters the Ouse above Goole, eighty-eight and a quarter miles.

ARKLE BECK.

Arkle Beck is the principal tributary of the Swale in Swaledale. It commences 1,275 feet above sea level at the junction of Beck Crooks and Annaside Becks, a little above Beck Crooks Bridge on the Reeth and Tanhill Highway, which runs parallel with the beck the whole of its course. These becks, the former of which is the principal, receive a number of small moorland tributaries which drain the Arkengarthdale Moors. The top reaches of Arkle Beck run through a wild moorland district, and receive the Roe Beck, and Great and Little Punchard Becks, whose gathering grounds lie between Arkengarthdale and Gunnerside Moors. After leaving the moors, the beck runs down a cultivated valley past Langthwaite and Reeth to the Swale, the other tributaries being of little importance. About half-a-mile above Eskleth Bridge, the hush from the lead mines on the moors near that place enters the Arkle, and the stream below suffers materially, the fishing being of little good; but above that point the trout fishing is good right away to the source, and the owners and tenants readily grant leave to fish. The close time is from September 1st to May 1st. Reeth, where there is good accommodation, is the best centre. A conveyance runs between Reeth and Richmond. The railway stations are Redmire, in Wensleydale, six miles; and Richmond, nine and a half miles. The confluence of Annaside Beck and Beck Crooks is just above Beck Crooks Bridge. These becks hold small trout. Two miles below Beck Crooks Bridge is New Bridge. There is a footbridge three-quarters of a mile lower down. Roe Beck enters just below. This beck holds some small trout. A mile and a quarter below New Bridge, the Punchard Becks enter. These becks also hold small trout. Whaw Bridge is half-a-mile below Punchard Becks end. A mile below Whaw Bridge is Low Eskleth, here the hush from the lead mines enters the Arkle. Eskleth Bridge is about half-a-mile below. Schoolhouse Bridge is a quarter of a mile still lower, and half-a-mile below Schoolhouse Bridge is Langthwaite Bridge. There is an inn at Langthwaite, and Arkle Town is a little lower down on the opposite side. Three miles and a quarter below Langthwaite Bridge is Reeth Mill Weir. Reeth Bridge is half-a-mile below the weir. Reeth stands between the two on the right bank. Fremington Mill Weir is just below Reeth Bridge, and half-a-mile below the bridge the Arkle enters the River Swale opposite Grinton. The total length of the stream is ten miles.

RIVER BAIN.

The River Bain runs from Lake Semmerwater to the Ure, at Bainbridge. The principal stream which feeds the lake rises at Bardale Head, 1,790 feet above the sea, and a little east of Dodd Fell. From the source to Marsett this moorland stream is called Bardale Beck, and receives several small mountain streams in its course. Below Marsett it is called Marsett Beck, for about half-a mile; then it becomes Crook Beck, until it reaches Lake Semmerwater. These streams all hold fish; but the fishing is in private hands, and the fish run somewhat small. Lake Semmer-water is almost two miles in circumference, the foot of the lake being near to the hamlet of Counterside. The fishing in the lake and in the River Bain is in the hands of the Wensleydale Angling Association. Hon sec., Mr. W. Balderstone, Yore Bridge House, Bainbridge, *via* Bedale. The best length of water belonging to this association is on the Ure. Annual subscription, 10s. 6d. Day tickets for outsiders, 2s. 6d. For full details see the River Ure *(post)*. Both trout and grayling. No coarse fish except in Lake Semmerwater, where there are quantities of rudd and bream. The fish in the lake, however, run only small, and are never well-fed like the fish in the Ure. The length of the Bain, from the lake to the River Ure, is two and a half miles. Bainbridge, which is a capital angling centre, stands at the junction of the two rivers. Askrigg Station is about three-quarters of a mile distant. There are good inns at both these places.

RIVER BALDER.

The River Balder is a tributary of the Tees, and has its source at the head of Baldersdale, which forms the valley between the Hunderthwaite and Cotherstone Moors. The river is formed by the junction of the Balder Beck and Blea Gill Beck, at Balder Head, 1,020 feet above sea level. The stream is bordered with trees almost its whole length. Baldersdale is best approached from Cotherstone, which is the nearest railway station. A little above Hury Mill there is a reservoir, belonging to the Stockton and Middlesbro' Waterworks, in course of construction. Above this reservoir the fishing is private. Below on the left bank there is half-a-mile of private water to New Scar. Below this to the Tees on the same side, the fishing belongs to Mr. T. Hutchinson, with the exception of one very short length of private water immediately above Cotherstone Bridge. Permission to fish Mr. Hutchinson's water can be had from his agent, Mr. Thos. Hill. For particulars see River Tees *(post)*. On the right side from the reservoir down to the Tees, permission to fish is easily obtained from the owners and tenants. The refuse and washings from the waterworks have affected the fishing in the Balder very considerably. Two miles below Balder Head is Blacktar Bridge. Two and three-quarter miles below this bridge is Hury Mill. The above mentioned reservoir is just above this mill. New Scar is half-a-mile below Hury Mill. A mile and three-quarters below New Scar the Teesdale Valley railway bridge crosses. Cotherstone Bridge is a mile lower down. At Cotherstone there are inns and a railway station. Half-a-mile below Cotherstone Bridge the Balder enters the Tees a little above Cotherstone Mill. The total length of the river is eight miles.

RIVER BURN.

The River Burn has its source on Masham Moors, 1,150 feet above sea level, and is formed by a number of small mountain streams which drain Colsterdale, Steel House, and Thorny Grain Moors. It runs in a north-easterly direction through a moorland district (three and a quarter miles) to Mark Bridge, Low House, where it is joined by Birk Gill Beck which runs from Caldbergh Moor. From Mark Bridge it turns east to Gollingwith Foot, and south-east to Leighton Bridge, receiving Spruce Gill Beck in its course. At five and a half miles below its source it receives Potter Beck, an important tributary, and thence it runs due east through a lovely country past Healey, and Swinton Park to Masham, entering the river Ure about one mile south of that place. Sole Beck and the streams from the lakes and fish ponds in Swinton Park are the tributaries on this length. The river has many windings, is a succession of pools and streams, holds a large quantity of fine trout, and is an ideal trout stream. Total length, ten miles. The fishing in this river is strictly private.

BURNISTON BECK.

This little stream, which is famous for its trout, rises at Skittles Slack, Scalby High Moor, on the Whitby Moors, 510 feet above sea level. In the first two miles and a quarter of its course it runs south and south-east to Lind Heads, and is known as Thirley Beck. At Lind Heads it receives two small streams, Grew Beck and Brown Beck, running due east to Cloughton Bridge, this portion of the stream being known as Lindhead Beck, and about a mile and a quarter in length. At Cloughton Bridge it receives Cloughton Beck, a small tributary, below which point it is called Burniston Beck, and runs south, past the village of Burniston to the east of Scalby Village, where it enters Scalby Beck. Burniston is half-a-mile below Cloughton Bridge ; from which bridge it is half-a-mile to Cloughton Station. Three-quarters of a mile lower down the Scarborough and Whitby Branch Railway crosses the stream. A mile below the railway bridge is Scalby Road Bridge ; a quarter of a mile below which the stream enters Scalby Beck. Total length of stream, six and a quarter miles. Over its whole course it is a succession of dubs and runs, and although it can be stepped across in most places it abounds with trout, many of them of good size. The best fishing is in the spring months. Above Lind Heads the fishing is not much good. From Lind Heads to Scalby Road

Bridge the stream is strictly preserved by the Burniston Angling Club with the exception of three fields above Cloughton Bridge, which are retained by the owners for their friends. The Burniston Angling Club was established March, 1893. President, the hon. F. Johnstone; vice-president, G. Hampton, Esq.; managing committee, Messrs. W. H. Allison, A. Lupton, J. E. Marsden, Rev. J. C. Simpson; hon. secretary and treasurer, J. E. Lupton, Harcourt Place, Scarborough; keeper, Hodson Sedman, Burniston. Limited to fourteen members. Annual subscription, £1 1s.; entrance fee, £1 1s. Season, March 16th to September 15th inclusive. Artificial fly only. No trout to be taken under 8in. No member allowed to fish more than two days in any one week. No member allowed to take more than ten brace of trout in one day. The keeper has power to examine any member's creel. As it is known there are chub in the stream members are allowed to fish for them with pith or paste from October 1st to March 1st inclusive.

THE CALDER.

The Calder rises at Calder Head, about one mile south of the Holme, in Lancashire. It is a small clear stream for the first mile of its course, when it receives the refuse from some cotton mills, and is very badly polluted a few miles lower down, at Todmorden, growing gradually worse as it runs through Sowerby Bridge, Elland, Brighouse, Dewsbury, and Wakefield, until it becomes an inky cesspool. It enters the River Aire at Castleford, forty-nine and a half miles from its source. The principal tributary is the Colne, which enters two and a half miles below Brighouse.

CLOUGH RIVER.

The source of the Clough River is formed 1,100 feet above sea level, about half-a-mile above Clough, by the confluence of the Grisdale and Ceaseat Becks. Grisdale Beck rises within a quarter of a mile of Rawthey Gill Foot, and is no inconsiderable stream, draining a large tract of moorland country lying between Holme

Moss Hill, the north-east side of Baugh Fell, and Grisdale Brow and Common. The Ceaseat Beck drains the south-east side of Baugh Fell. The Clough River below Clough runs the whole of its course to the Rawthey down a deep valley, shut in by high hills and mountains, from which fall multitudinous small streams, which drain the south side of Baugh Fell and the north side of Rise Hill. The Sedbergh and Kirkby Stephen highway runs parallel with the river the whole of its course. Sedbergh, where there is accommodation and a railway station, is the best centre. There is nothing but trout in this stream, but they are found in the whole of its length, and the whole of the fishing from end to end is practically open. Anglers who conduct themselves properly are not molested. Trout licences, 2s. 6d. Other restrictions in accordance with the Fisheries Board Regulations. River watcher, William Holmes, High Oaks, Sedbergh. Clough Bridge is three-quarters of a mile below the source. Hard Ing Bridge is a quarter of a mile lower, and High Scale Bridge, Low Scale Bridge, and Kundsman Bridge all come within the next quarter of a mile. Half-a-mile below Kundsman Bridge is Holland's or Ing's Head Bridge, and Scar Foot Bridge is a quarter of a mile lower. Three-quarters of a mile below Scar Foot is Bank's Bridge, Mill Bridge coming in between. A mile below is Kirk Bridge, Ben's Bridge coming in between. Half-a-mile still lower is Low House Bridge. Three-quarters of a mile below Low House Bridge is Winterscales Bridge, with Aye Gill Bridge between. Bridge End is half-a-mile below, and New Bridge a quarter of a mile still lower. Danny Bridge is a mile below New Bridge, and a mile and three-quarters below Danny Bridge is Garsdale Bridge and Mill. A quarter of a mile above the bridge is Far Field Weir, and just below the bridge the stream enters the River Rawthey. The total length of Clough River is nine miles.

RIVER COCK.

The River Cock rises about one mile north-east of Seacroft, 275 feet above sea level, and is but a small beck for the first three and a quarter miles of its course, when it becomes the chief feeder of the lake in Parlington Park. From Parlington it runs east of Barwick to Aberford, thence across the memorable Towton Field, north-west of the village of Saxton, past Sutton Village, and north of Grimston Park, where it enters the Wharfe three-quarters of a mile below Tadcaster Bridge. It is a very irregular and circuitous stream, running through a somewhat flat country; but it holds some fairly decent fish and might with cultivation be made into a good angling stream. The whole of the fishing that is worth anything is in private hands. The total length of the stream is sixteen miles.

CODBECK.

The source of Codbeck is the overflow from High Dam Reservoir, 650 feet above sea level, situate on Hither Moor, which is part of the Osmotherly Moors. High Dam is fed by Crabdale Beck, which receives Langdale and Ingdale Becks, all of which run from the Osmotherly Moors, which lie on the north-west side of the Cleveland Hills. The stream runs west to Foxton, and thence due south by Thirsk and Topcliffe to the Swale, through a somewhat undulating country. Codbeck is a very good angling stream, holding some large trout, and being fishable from source to mouth. Thirsk is the best centre.

From the source to Brawith Bridge, twelve and a quarter miles, the fishing is private on both sides. At High Mill, a mile below the source, there are three dams holding fish. Half-a-mile lower down there is a bridge, on the low side of which is a weir. From this point it is a quarter of a mile to Osmotherly. A quarter of a mile below is Osmotherly Bridge, and half-a-mile lower down are Bog Hole Bridge and Long Bridge, from which it is three-quarters of a mile to Thimbleby. There are two dams just below Long Bridge. Walk Mill Bridge is a mile below Long Bridge. There is a weir just below the bridge, and Ellerbeck Bridge is a quarter of a mile lower down. Ellerbeck is half-a-mile below the bridge. From Ellerbeck the highway runs parallel with the stream to Thirsk. A mile below Ellerbeck, Howl Beck enters just above Foxton Mills. Sigston Bridge is a mile and a quarter below Howl

Beck end. About a quarter of a mile below here the stream enters a narrow valley, whose sloping, wooded sides fall to a narrow glade, through which the stream runs to Cotcliffe Bridge, which is two and three-quarter miles below Sigston Biidge. Crosby Bridge is three-quarters of a mile below Cotcliffe Bridge. It is a mile and a quarter to Thornton-le-Beans. Carr Bridge is a quarter of a mile lower down, from which it is three-quarters of a mile to Borrowby. A mile and a half below Carr Bridge, Broad Beck enters. This is a private trout stream. From this point it is a mile and a quarter to Thornton-le-Moor, and two miles to Otterington station. A quarter of a mile below there is a bridge, from which it is a mile and three-quarters to Knayton. Brawith Bridge is half-a-mile lower down. There are inns at all the above places.

From Brawith Bridge to Spittle Beck end, Major Mott, of Kilvington Hall, Thirsk, grants day tickets, on application, to fish both sides of the stream, and also the north side of Spittle Beck which holds some nice trout. Nothing but fly and minnow allowed. The south side of Spittle Beck is private. There is a weir a quarter of a mile below Brawith Bridge. Thornton-le-Street, where there is an inn, is almost a mile below the bridge. Kilvington Old Hall is a mile below Thornton-le-Street, and Spittle Beck enters the stream a quarter of a mile below that.

From Spittle Beck to the river Swale, the fishing is in the hands of the Thirsk Angling Club, president, R. Bell, Esq.; hon. sec., Mr. Jos. Ellerby, Thirsk. This club was only formed last season. Members must reside within a radius of five miles of Thirsk. Annual subscription, 2s. 6d. Any member paying 5s. is entitled to one ordinary and one transferable ticket, and 10s. two transferable tickets. Close time for trout, Oct. 2nd to April 1st. Limit for trout, 8in. All rods and landing nets to be marked with that length. No dogs allowed. No fishing between 9 p.m. and 6 a.m., except in June, July, and August, when fishing is allowed up to 10 p.m. No Sunday fishing allowed. Panniers to be shown when challenged. Owners and tenants have one ordinary, and one or more transferable tickets. About Thirsk and above, trout only. Below Thirsk, chiefly grayling and other coarse fish. Both trout and grayling very good. South Kilvington, where there are inns, is a mile below Spittle Beck. Thirsk is a mile and a quarter below South Kilvington. First-class accommodation for anglers, sportsmen, and tourists, and full information about the fishing, can be had at W. Hall's, Golden Fleece Hotel, Thirsk. One mile to the railway station. Lock Bridge is half-a-mile below Mill Bridge, Thirsk. Blakey Bridge is a quarter of a mile lower down. Sowerby stands on the right bank. Here there are inns. Town End Bridge is a quarter of a mile below Blakey Bridge, and the York and Newcastle railway bridge crosses a mile and a quarter lower down. A mile and a half below the railway bridge is Dalton. Here there is an inn, and it is one mile to Sessay station. Fisher Beck, Isles Beck, and Dalton Beck enter Codbeck at Dalton. These streams hold some good fish, but the fishing in them is private. A mile and a quarter below Dalton is Dalton Bridge, near Topcliffe. There are inns at Topcliffe, and it is two and a quarter miles to the railway station. Manor House Bridge is three quarters of a mile below Dalton Bridge, and a quarter of a mile lower down, Codbeck enters the river Swale, opposite Leckby Carr, about one and a half miles below Topcliffe. The total length of Codbeck is twenty-three and a half miles. The Board of Conservators turned a large quantity of yearling trout into this stream at the commencement of the present season.

RIVER COLNE.

The River Colne is formed by numerous streams which drain the Marsden Moors, the two principal being Haigh Clough and Redbrook Clough, which run from Haigh and Redbrook Reservoirs respectively. The river starts about one and a quarter miles above Marsden and immediately after its formation enters Waterside Reservoir, which is the feeder for the Huddersfield Canal, which runs parallel with the river. The Colne runs through Marsden, Slaithwaite, Milnsbridge, Huddersfield (ten miles from source), and Colnbridge, where it enters the River Calder, opposite Cooper Bridge Station. The canal also enters the Calder at the same point. The total length of the Colne is thirteen and three-quarter miles. This river is polluted, and no good for angling purposes, but some of its higher tributaries feed the Longwood Top and Bottom Reservoirs and the Compensation Reservoir, which have their gathering grounds on Longwood Moors; and another tributary of the Colne, which enters below Huddersfield, feeds the Woodside Reservoir. The principal tributary of the Colne is the River Holme (see *post*). Longwood Top Reservoir, which contains pike and perch, is eight acres in extent, and 700 feet above sea level. The Bottom Reservoir, pike, perch, &c., is three and a half acres in extent, and has an altitude of 630 feet; and the Compensation Reservoir, perch, roach, &c., is eight and a half acres, and 575 feet above the sea. These reservoirs are three miles from Huddersfield, the nearest railway station being Longwood. The Woodside Reservoir, trout and roach, is one and a half acres in extent, 350 feet above the sea, and two miles from Huddersfield. The fishing in these reservoirs, and likewise in the Blackmoorfoot, Deerhill, Holmstyes, Bawshaw, and Blacksike Reservoirs, which are in the River Holme watershed (see *post*), is in the hands of the Huddersfield Angling Association; president, Mr. W. P. Hellawell; hon. secretary, Thomas Tuley, Albion Street, Huddersfield; treasurer, Mr. J. J. Vickers. The membership is limited to one hundred. Entrance fee, 21s.; annual subscription, 10s. 6d. Any member selling his fish, or refusing to show his ticket or basket when challenged, forfeits the same. Honorary members paying 21s. annually, have the privilege of taking a friend. Outsiders' daily tickets, 2s. 6d.; weekly tickets, 5s.; to be had from the secretaries. Limit for pike at Longwood Reservoirs, 18in. Limit for perch at Longwood and Blackmoorfoot Reservoirs, 8in. No dogs allowed. At Blackmoorfoot and Longwood Top and Bottom Reservoirs, a register is kept in which all members must sign their names before proceeding to fish. No member allowed to fish more than two days a week in any of these three mentioned reservoirs. Limit for trout, 9in. Close time for Blackmoorfoot, Longwood, and Deerhill Reservoirs, March 14th to June 16th; for Holmstyes, Bawshaw, Woodside, and Blacksike Reservoirs, September 30th to April 1st.

RIVER COSTA.

The River Costa has its source at Keld Head, about three-quarters of a mile west of Pickering, 96 feet above sea level. A geological "fault" brings the Kimmerage clay in the Derwent Valley sharply into juxtaposition with the underlying oolitic rocks out-cropping on the high ground to the north. The water gathering and percolating through these rocks is choked in its course by the clay, and finds an outlet in a large volume at Keld. A characteristic feature of the stream is that the temperature is never lower than 37 degs., owing to the great depth it travels underground. Thus it rises to the surface many degrees higher than the surrounding temperature, and therefore never freezes. It is this high temperature which hastens the growth of aquatic weeds in the Costa which are such a nuisance to anglers. The bed of the river is mostly of a muddy and peaty bottom, overlying a thin seam of gravel, upon which the Kimmerage clay here and there bursts through. Pickering Beck enters the river about half way down its course. The lower part becomes sluggish, and is more suited to coarse fish.

The trout fishing in the Mayfly season is exceptionally good, trout averaging 1½lb. to 2lb. But the Costa is *par excellence* a grayling stream. Few rivers in any county excel it either in size, quality, or abundance The fish are shy, owing to the placid nature of the stream and the abundance of crustacean food.

Almost the whole of the Costa is strictly preserved by the Costa Anglers' Club, limited to forty members. President, Richard Hill, Esq., Sinnington; hon. secretary, Mr. J. H. Philips, 22, Albermarle Crescent, Scarborough. No short period tickets issued. Annual subscription, £3 3s., with £4 4s. entrance fee. No member allowed to fish for trout more than twenty days each year; only one rod allowed. Limit for trout, 9in. Bait permitted: artificial fly, artificial and natural minnow. Close time for trout, October 2nd to April 16th inclusive. Grayling may be taken throughout the year; no Sunday fishing. Dogs prohibited. Keepers have power to examine baskets and tickets and to seize unlawful implements and instruments of capture. No person allowed to kill more than ten brace of trout per day. This does not extend to grayling. Every member expected to take out a fishing licence, and produce it and his ticket of membership when requested by the keeper. Watchers, T. B. Metcalfe, Keld Head, Pickering; James Pool, Kirby Misperton, Pickering.

The Costa Anglers' Club length extends from the source to Harding's Plantation, both sides of the river, six and a half miles. Keld Head is three-quarters of a mile from Pickering, where there are several inns and a railway station. Kirby Misperton Park and fish pond are four miles below the source. Kirby Misperton Bridge is four and three-quarter miles below the source. Just above the bridge Pickering Beck enters. This is an important angling stream (see *post*). There is an inn at Kirby Misperton. Harding's Plantation is a mile and three-quarters below Kirby Misperton Bridge. The nearest railway station is Marishes Road, one and three-quarter miles.

The Costa Club length ends at Harding's Plantation, and the remainder of the fishing in the Costa on the right side is in the hands of the owners and tenants, from whom permission must be obtained. The left side belongs to the newly-formed Lower Costa Angling Club, president, G. Hampton, Esq., Scalby; hon. secretary, J. E. Lupton, Esq., Scarborough. The club is limited to ten members, and is strictly of a private character. No short season tickets are issued. Close time and regulations in accordance with the Yorkshire Fishery Board. Limit for trout, 9in.; grayling and pike any size. The length holds some fine trout and grayling, and a few pike and perch.

From Harding's Plantation to the confluence with the River Rye it is three miles. The Costa enters the Rye at Howe Bridge, where the Malton and Pickering highway crosses. Malton is the nearest railway station, three miles and a half. The total length of the stream is nine and a half miles.

RIVER COVER.

The River Cover rises 1,600 feet above the sea, near Grouse House, on Cover Head Moor, which lies north-west of Great Whernside and only about a mile from the source of the River

Nidd, which runs down the adjoining valley. In its highest reaches, the Cover drains the north-west sides of Great and Little Whernside and the Cowside and Coverdale Moors. These are high, barren, moorland districts, and the small streams falling to the river are very numerous, and after a heavy rainfall carry a great volume of water to the main stream. From Kettlewell, in Wharfedale, there is a highway which runs over the moor and down Coverdale to Middleham. It is three miles from Coverhead to Kettlewell, from which place it is fifteen miles to Skipton, the nearest railway station. For the lower part of the river, which runs along a charming valley past Carlton, Coverham Abbey, and Middleham, to the Ure at Cover Bridge, Leyburn is the best railway communication.

This is a very good angling stream, all trout. The salmon getting up the river too late in the season to be of much use for angling purposes. In heavy freshes the salmon get to the highest reaches, but they are not very plentiful. The fishing is all private, but from the source down to West Scrafton leave is not difficult to obtain from the owners and tenants. Below West Scrafton to the Ure the Cover is preserved, but permission is occasionally granted. From the source to Hunter's Hall Bridge, it is two and three-quarter miles. Here the Middleham and Kettlewell highway crosses the stream. Three and a quarter miles below is Horsehouse, where there is an inn. Two miles and a half below Horsehouse is Nathwaite Bridge. Wide of the river is Carlton, and half-a-mile lower down is West Scrafton. Inns at both places. St. Simon's Bridge is a mile and a half below Nathwaite Bridge, and Coverham Bridge is two miles still lower. Low Mill and Weir are half-a-mile below Coverham Bridge. From this point it is one mile to Middleham. A mile below Coverham Bridge is Hullo Bridge, and two miles below Hullo Bridge is Cover Bridge. East Witton stands wide of the river. It is two miles from Middleham to Leyburn Station. It is two miles from Cover Bridge to Spennithorne Station. There are inns at these places. A quarter of a mile below Cover Bridge the river enters the Ure, near to Batts Island, below Ulshaw Bridge. The total length of the Cover is fifteen and a half miles.

RIVER CRIMPLE.

The Crimple rises 785 feet above sea level on Stainburn Moor, a little west of Crimple Head House and south of Haverah Park. About one mile from its source it crosses the Dudley Hill and Killinghall T.P. Road, near to Shawfield Head. Here it is a mere mountain rivulet, but below Hole House it receives Bull Dike and assumes more importance, running with many windings past Burnt Bridge and Pannal to Almsford Bridge, receiving in its course many small tributaries. From Almsford Bridge it runs through a circuitous vale past Rudding Park, Collins Bridge, Guilders Bridge, and Spofforth, where it enters a comparatively flat country, until it enters the River Nidd opposite Ribston Park. The principal tributaries in the lower reaches are Hookstone Beck, Townend Beck, the overflow from Plompton Lake, Park Beck, and Stockeld Beck. It is a meandering stream throughout, running through a picturesque country, and is an ideal trout stream holding some good fish and affording capital sport.

From the source to Almsford Bridge the fishing is preserved by the Harrogate Angling Association, composed of twenty-five honorary and twenty-five ordinary members. President, Mr. Riley Fortune, F.Z.S.; vice-president, Mr. T. Laycock; hon. secretary, Mr. C. Allen, Cathcart House, Harrogate; hon. assistant secretary, Mr. A. Rowling; hon. treasurer, G. Morrell; river watchers, John Temple, —Hardcastle, Beckwithshaw. Annual subscription for honorary members, 10s. 6d., the ticket being transferable to a non-resident friend. Ordinary members, 6s. yearly, which includes trout license. Day tickets for outsiders, 4s., obtainable from the secretary. Limit for trout, 7in. Rods to be marked with that length. All illegal fishing or medicated baits prohibited. Close time according to the Regulations of the Yorkshire Fishery Board. All creels to be open to inspection. Anglers are cautioned against breaking down fences or trees, or otherwise doing damage, and neglecting to fasten gates after passing through. The club have recently put five hundred fine trout into their water. They have also a long stretch of water in Oak Beck (see *post*) and on the Ure at Borougbridge (see *post*). This is the club's first season.

The above mentioned T.P. road crosses the stream one mile below the source, from which point it is four miles to Harrogate and six miles to Otley. Shaw Green Bridge crosses a mile lower down and Burnt Bridge two miles and a half still lower down. From Burnt Bridge it is two and three-quarter miles to Harrogate. Pannal Bridge is half-a-mile below Burnt Bridge and Almsford Bridge half-a-mile below Pannal Bridge. Almsford Bridge is two miles from Harrogate on the Leeds and Harrogate highway.

Below Almsford Bridge to the Bleach Works, about three-quarters of a mile, the fishing is very good, but it is strictly private. Below the Bleach Works it falls off somewhat until nearing Spofforth. On this length down to Guilders Bridge the fishing is in the hands of the tenants, from whom permission must be obtained. Below Guilders Bridge and Spofforth it improves, about Ribston being very good. Both trout and grayling beside coarse fish. From Guilders Bridge to Spofforth Mill the water has been leased for five years by the Harrogate Conservative Angling Club. The club have also fishing rights on Oak Beck, the Rivers Ure and Nidd. For particulars see Oak Beck *(post)*. Below Spofforth to the Nidd the fishing is private.

Hookstone Beck enters at seven miles from the source. Rudding Park is half-a-mile lower down. Collins Bridge is a mile below Hookstone Beck. From this bridge it is two and a quarter miles to Harrogate. A mile and a quarter below Collins Bridge is Guilders Bridge. From this bridge it is half-a-mile to Plompton Rocks and Follifoot, where there in an inn. Townend Beck enters a quarter of a mile below Guilders Bridge and Plompton Beck half-a-mile still lower. Park Beck enters a quarter of a mile below Plompton Beck. A quarter of a mile lower down there is a weir, and Spofforth Bridge is half-a-mile below. There is an inn at Spofforth. Stockeld Beck enters a mile below the bridge and three-quarters of a mile below the beck is Stock or Newsham Bridge. A mile and a half below Newsham Bridge is Ribston Bridge. From this bridge it is four miles to Wetherby and three miles to Knaresbro'. Inns and railway stations at both places. The Crimple enters the Nidd a mile and a quarter below Ribston Bridge, opposite Ribston Park. Total length fifteen and a half miles.

RIVER DEARN.

The River Dearn rises at Dearn Spring, 1,100 feet above sea level, on Dearn Common, Foolstone Moors, east of Holmfirth. It commences to be polluted by refuse from the dye works, two and a half miles below its source, thus for angling purposes this part of the river is no good. These pollutions however settle somewhat before they reach Cawthorne Dike, which joins the Dearn eleven miles below its source. This dike runs from the fish ponds in Canon Hall Park, which are well stocked with trout, but the fishing is private. In Cawthorne Dike and from the dike end in the Dearn down to near Barnsley are found chub, roach, pike, perch, and gudgeon, and an occasional trout, but permission to fish both the dike and the river must be had from the landowners. After a freshet plenty of fish can be taken. Below Barnsley, which is fourteen and a half miles from the source, the pollutions recommence and gradually get worse; thus there is an end to the fishing for the remainder of the river. From Barnsley, the river flows past Darfield, Wath, Bolton, and Ardwick to the River Don, which it enters about half-a-mile above Conisborough. The total length of the river is thirty-one and a half miles.

The principal tributary of the Dearn is the Dove (see *post*), which enters below Darfield twenty-three miles from the source. Knoll Beck was formerly an important angling tributary, but it is now a feeder of the Elsecar branch of the Dearn and Dove Canal. This canal holds some good fish. The beck runs from Elsecar Reservoir, which is about half-a-mile north of Wentworth. The reservoir holds some good fish. Permission to fish the same can be had from Earl Fitzwilliam's agent, Wentworth. The branch canal from Elsecar to the Dearn and Dove is practically open fishing, being in the hands of the owners and tenants, who do not interfere so long as anglers conduct themselves properly. Pike, eels, roach, chub, and bream.

RIVER DEE.

The source of the Dee is formed at Dale Head by the confluence of Fell End Gill and Long Gill Becks, moorland streams which receive a number of smaller streams, and drain the north side of Blea Moor, which lies east of Whernside. Immediately after its source it runs down Dent Dale, a charming Yorkshire valley which is bordered by high mountains. The stream receives numberless small tributaries which fall from the north side of Whernside and Lord's Land, and from the south side of Lord's Hill. The principal tributary is Deepdale Beck, which holds a quantity of fish, and is open fishing. All the tributary streams, or runners as they are locally called, hold small fish from the head of the dale downwards. Nothing but trout and salmon, and the latter can get up the river as far as Hell's Cauldron Waterfall, which is only about three miles and a half below the source. From the source to Holme Barn Bridge the fishing is practically free so long as anglers do no damage. From Holme Barn Bridge to Rash Mill Weir the water is private on both sides, and below to the River Rawthey the fishing is open again on both sides. Salmon licences, 20s. ; trout, 2s. 6d. Restrictions in accordance with the Fisheries Board Regulations. Close time: salmon, November 15th to March 1st; trout, October 2nd to March 1st. River watcher, William Holmes, High Oaks, Sedbergh. Dent Station on the Settle and Carlisle Railway is the nearest station for the top end of the river, and Sedbergh for the bottom. Dent and Sedbergh are the best centres. Good accommodation at both places. Stone House Bridge is a mile below Dale Head, and Cow Dub Bridge a quarter of a mile still lower. Here there is an inn. Half-a-mile below Cow Dub is Harbour Gill Bridge, from which it is half-a-mile to Dent Station. From this point the highway runs parallel with the river the whole of its course. Half-a-mile below Harbour Gill, Cowgill Beck, which holds fish, enters. Ewegales Bridge is at this point; there is a waterfall and Hud's Force just below. Helms Bridge is half-a-mile below Cowgill Beck, and Hell's Cauldron Waterfall is about a mile lower down, Nelly's Bridge coming in between. Hacker Gill Beck, which holds fish, enters at this point. Half-a-mile below the waterfall is Tommy Bridge, and Deepdale Beck enters half-a-mile still lower. Three-quarters of a mile below Deepdale Beck is Church Bridge, and the village of Dent stands on the left bank. Barth Bridge is a mile lower down, and Holme Barn Bridge a mile lower still. Oliver's Beck and Wilsey Beck enter between these two bridges. Two miles below Holme Barn Bridge is Rash Bridge; the mill and weir are just below. A mile below Rash Bridge is Amit Holme Bridge, and the Dee enters the Rawthey just below. The total length of the river is eleven miles. The river is of greater width and volume than its length suggests, on account of the great amount of drainage it carries off from the surrounding mountains.

RIVER DERWENT.

The River Derwent rises 880 feet above the sea a short distance from the shooting box on Derwent Head or High Woof Howe on Wykeham High Moor. In the first four miles of its course it is nothing more than an inconsiderable mountain stream running through bare moorlands and receiving some minor streams. The first important tributary is Harwood Dale Beck, which receives in its course the Jugger Howe, Raven Gill, Helwath and Castle Becks, which run from the Fylingdales and Harwood Dale Moors. The next tributary is Black Beck, which gathers waters from Bickly Heights and Bickly Moor, and receiving the Cross Cliffe Beck, a continuation of Black and Grain Becks, which drain the north side of Allerston and Lockton High and Low Moors. Other streams which fall into Black Beck are Deepdale, Stockland, and Hipperley Becks, which drain the Ebberstone Moors. The Troutsdale Beck drains Troutsdale and Brampton Moors, and the above, with the streams flowing from the series of valleys about Hackness Park, form the chief gathering grounds of the Upper Derwent. The course of the river is somewhat peculiar. It runs through Forge Valley and Ayton, as if it meant thus early to end its career in the sea wide of Scarborough, when it turns suddenly to the west and enters upon the vales of Pickering and York to the Ouse. For over thirty miles of its course there are no other tributaries of importance, unless it be the New Hertford River. Then the Thornton Beck, and lower still the River Rye, enter, the latter being the chief tributary of the Derwent. Below the confluence of the Rye the tributary streams are unimportant, so that for more than one half of its length the river does not increase in size, the lower reaches being very narrow and confined.

The angling on the Derwent embraces all kinds of fish, and has the reputation of being good throughout, considering the variety of fishing. The best trout lengths are on the Upper Derwent, the best water being in the hands of the Derwent Anglers' Club, which is, however, fishable by ticket. The trout length on the river extends from the source to the bottom limit of Sir Charles Legard's water, below Yedingham, although fine trout are caught as low down the river as Kirkham and Howsham. There is excellent fishing in the middle reaches of the Derwent. Both game and coarse fish, the latter being plentiful. Below Howsham and Buttercrambe to the mouth of the river, pike, chub, dace, bream, eels, in fact, all kinds of coarse fish, abound. Possibly the Lower Derwent is the best length of coarse fishing in Yorkshire. The salmon fishing is also good, but this is all strictly private, the best of it being in the hands of Messrs. Aspinall & Masterman, fish and game dealers, Coney Street, York. The salmon fishing is confined to the lower reaches: they rarely get above Sutton Weir. Most of the coarse fishing and some of the trout fishing is open to the public, either by ticket or permission from tenants and owners, which is easily obtained. The highest railway station on the Upper Derwent is Forge Valley. From the source and in the mountain tributaries as far as the confluence of Black Beck the fishing is free. There is a plentiful supply of fish in these moorland streams, but they run only small. Black Beck enters near Broxa, just below Langdale Bridge, eight miles from the source. From Black Beck to Hilla Green Bridge, about three-quarters of a mile, is the private fishing of Capt. the Hon. Francis Johnstone, of Hackness.

From Hilla Green Bridge the Derwent Anglers' Club length extends on both sides the river to Hertford Dale, East and West Ayton Ings, ten and three-quarter miles without a break. Prince's Mill, Ayton Bridge, divides the upper and the lower waters. The upper water is best for trout and grayling; the lower water, besides trout and grayling, contains pike, chub, dace, and eels. The fishing throughout the club length is excellent. Club officials:

patron, the Earl of Londesborough; president, Lord Derwent; vice-president, Capt. the Hon. F. Johnstone; treasurers, Messrs. Woodhall, Hebden, & Co.; hon. secretary, T. B. Etty, Esq., Grosvenor Villa, Scarborough. River watchers, William Wardell and Samuel Monkman, East Ayton. Limited to forty members. Annual subscription, £2 10s.; entrance fee, £3 3s. On the written recommendation of a member, day tickets for the upper water can be had, except in May or June, on application to Mr. Clarke, 44, Huntriss Row, Scarborough: price, 5s. Under similar recommendation, season tickets can be had: price, £4 4s. Persons using these tickets must fish in strict accordance with the club rules. Every angler is expected to have his ticket with him and to show the same when challenged. Day tickets for the lower water, 2s. 6d. Members and ticket-holders are entitled to fish between sunrise and sunset as follows: for trout, with artificial fly only, from April 15th to September 30th inclusive; and for grayling, with artificial fly only, from April 15th to March 14th inclusive, over all the club water. In the lower water, below Prince's Mill, Ayton, with any bait except medicated bait and salmon spawn, for trout, from June 17th to September 30th; and for grayling and coarse fish, from June 17th to March 14th. Fishing for trout with minnow in the upper water, from Weir Head to Hilla Green Bridge, is allowed from July 1st to August 12th. Any member fishing more than thirty days in one season for trout, to pay 2s. 6d. per day for each additional day. Limit for trout, eight inches; limit for grayling in the lower water, eight inches. Keepers have power to inspect panniers and measure all fish. Not more than ten brace of trout per day to be taken on the upper water, but grayling may be taken on this length without regard to size or number. Not more than ten brace of trout or grayling to be taken from the lower water in one day. Fishing for chub with pith allowed from November 1st to January 31st on both waters. No dogs or wading allowed. The club have recently turned 500 Lough Neagh trout and 40,000 fry into their water, to which the Yorkshire Fishery Board have added 1,000 yearlings. The club have also turned 400 mature perch into the lower water. Hackness is a mile and a half below Hilla Green Bridge. Here there is an inn, the nearest railway station being Scalby, three and three-quarter miles. Forge Valley commences just below Hackness. Everley is a mile below Hackness. The cut to Scalby Beck (see *post*) leaves the river about a quarter of a mile lower down. Forge Valley ends about a quarter of a mile above Ayton, which is four and three-quarter miles below Hackness. There are inns and a railway station at Ayton. It is four and three-quarter miles to Scarborough. The length of the lower portion of the Derwent Club water, from Ayton Bridge to East and West Ayton Ings, is four and a half miles.

At Ayton Ings Sir Chas. Legard's private water commences, and extends for about two miles down the river. Below this private length to Yedingham Bridge the fishing on both sides of the river is in the hands of the owners and tenants, from whom permission may be obtained. It is readily granted about Yedingham and Foulbridge, so long as anglers keep out of the crops. New Hertford river enters a mile and three-quarters below Ayton Ings. Hay Bridge crosses immediately below. From Hay Bridge to Ganton Station it is a quarter of a mile, and to Ganton village one mile. Here there are inns. Brompton Bridge is two and a quarter miles below Hay Bridge. Brompton village is one and a half miles from the Bridge. There are inns and a railway station. Sherburn is a mile and three quarters wide of the river. Brompton Beck enters a mile below the Bridge. Here the cut commences, which runs parallel with the river to Yedingham Bridge. Half a mile below Brompton Beck is Foulbridge. Snainton is a mile and three-quarters wide of the river. Inn and railway station. Yedingham Bridge is two and a half miles below Foulbridge. There is an inn. It is one and a half miles to Heslerton Station on the one hand, and one and three-quarter miles to Wilton Station on the other.

The fishing from Yedingham Bridge to the railway bridge, where the Whitby and Pickering Branch crosses the river below Scampton Bogs, is private on the left side, and on the opposite side in the hands of the tenants, from whom permission may be obtained. Heslerton Station is one and a half miles wide of Yedingham Bridge. Skelton Ferry is three and a half miles below

Yedingham Bridge. Knapton Station is two miles from Skelton Ferry wide of the river. Whitby and Pickering Railway Bridge is five and a half miles below Yedingham Bridge.

From the railway bridge to Rye Mouth on both sides of the river permission must be had from the tenants. The members of the Leeds Royal Exchange Angling Society have a standing permit to fish this part of the Derwent. President, Alderman Alf Cook, Esq. ; vice-president, Mr. T. Moss ; hon. secretary, Mr. T. W. Fishburn, Covered Market, Leeds. Limited to 100 members. Entrance fee, 5s. ; annual subscription, 5s. No short period tickets. Limit for trout and grayling, 7in. Mr. Cartwright, the landlord of the inn at Schoolhouse Hill, can also grant permission to anglers to fish the same length. Schoolhouse Hill is a short mile below the railway bridge. At Schoolhouse Hill there is a foot bridge across the river, from which it is one mile and three-quarters to Rillington Station. Rye Mouth is one and a half miles below Schoolhouse Hill.

The River Rye (see *post*), which is the main tributary of the Derwent and an important angling stream, enters the Derwent at this point. The New Cut also commences here, and runs on the right side parallel with the river to Malton Mill. The fishing on the right side from Rye Mouth to the Gannock at Old Malton belongs to Earl Fitzwilliam, but free tickets can be had to fish this water on application to his lordship's agent, Gervase Markham, Esq., Fitzwilliam Estate Offices, Old Maltongate, Malton. The ticket also allows the holder to fish a considerable portion of the Rye from Swinton Drain to the Derwent, and is available for one season, which ends on the 14th of March each year. No dogs allowed. All persons found fishing without a ticket will be prosecuted. The ticket is liable to be cancelled at any time (this in cases where anglers misconduct themselves), and must be shown when requested. Rod and line only. All legitimate baits. No Sunday fishing. Coarse fish are plentiful. Pike, chub, roach, dace, eels, grayling, and a few trout. Mr. John Anderson, fishing tackle dealer, 52, Market Place, Malton, is glad to afford anglers any information. Mr. Anderson is also appointed by the Yorkshire Fishery Board distributor of trout licenses for Malton district.

(see page 158). On the opposite, or left side of the river, the fishing from Rye Mouth to Norton Bridge is in the hands of owners and tenants, from whom permission is needed. From Rye Mouth to Norton Bridge the towing-path runs on the right bank. From Rye Mouth to Old Malton is three and a half miles. Here there are several inns. The Gannock is about a quarter of a mile below Old Malton, and Norton or Malton Bridge about one mile. At Norton and Malton there are numerous inns and a railway station. The lower bridge and Malton Station are about a quarter of a mile below Norton Bridge.

From Norton Bridge the fishing is open on the left bank to Kirkham Park boundary. The towing-path also runs down this side to Kirkham Bridge. On the right side to Cram Beck, which is the top boundary of the Castle Howard estate, permission is needed from owners and tenants. Huttons Ambo Station and suspension bridge are three and a quarter miles below Malton. Menethorpe, where there is an inn, is on the opposite bank of the river. Cram Beck is two and a quarter miles below the suspension bridge. At Cram Beck the Castle Howard estate commences, and from this point to Howsham Bridge the fishing is private on the right side of the river. Castle Howard Station is a quarter of a mile below Cram Beck, and Kirkham Park boundary half-a-mile. From this point to Howsham Bridge the fishing is private on the left side of the river. The fishing about Kirkham is very good. Kirkham Bridge is three-quarters of a mile below Castle Howard Station. There is a railway station at Kirkham. Kirkham Weir and Lock are about a quarter of a mile below the bridge. Howsham Bridge is about three miles below Kirkham. Howsham Locks and Weir are a little above the bridge. From Howsham Bridge it is a mile and a half to Barton-le-Willows, and two and a quarter miles to Barton Hill Station. There are inns at both places.

From Howsham Bridge to opposite Evers Beck the fishing on the right side is in the hands of the tenants, from whom permission must be had. Below it is private to Buttercambe Bridge. On the left side the towing-path runs from Howsham Bridge to Stamford Bridge, and permission to fish on this side may be had from the tenants for the water extending from

Howsham Bridge to opposite Aldby Park boundary. Below that point it is private to Buttercrambe Bridge. It is two miles from Howsham Bridge to Evers Beck. Scrayingham is just below Evers Beck. The nearest railway station is Stamford Bridge. Aldby Park boundary is a mile below Evers Beck on the opposite side. Buttercrambe Bridge is a mile and three-quarters below Evers Beck. There is a weir at Buttercrambe Bridge, also a lock and weir just above the bridge. Stamford Bridge is the nearest railway station, two and a half miles.

From Buttercrambe Bridge to Stamford Bridge, two and three-quarter miles, the tenant of Aldby Park has the fishing along with his tenancy, but he willingly grants permission to all *bonâ fide* anglers who conduct themselves in a sportsmanlike manner. The nearest railway station to Buttercrambe is Stamford Bridge, two and a half miles. At Stamford Bridge there is a lock and weir, and several inns. The bridge stands on the highway to York.

The towing-path runs down the right side of the river from Stamford Bridge to Kexby Bridge. The fishing about Stamford Bridge is very good, pike, chub, dace, bream, in fact, all kinds of coarse fish abounding. On the left side, from Stamford Bridge to Low Catton, permission to fish is readily granted by the tenants, and from Low Catton to Kexby Bridge permission can be had from Lord Leckonfield's steward. On the right side it is private from Stamford Bridge to Catton Reach, and below to Kexby Bridge permission can be had from Lord Londesborough's steward, Mr. Stephen Young, Scoreby, York.

Low Catton, where there is an inn, is a mile and a quarter below Stamford Bridge. Kexby Bridge is a mile and a quarter below Low Catton. The nearest railway station to Kexby is Stamford Bridge. It is six and a half miles by the highway to York.

From Kexby Bridge to Sutton Weir, about three miles, permission to fish can be had from the tenants on both sides of the river. At Newton-upon-Derwent, which is a mile wide of the river, there is an inn. Elvington stands on the right side of Sutton Bridge, and Sutton-upon-Derwent on the left. There are inns at both places. There is a weir, lock, and salmon ladder just below the bridge. Sutton is a favourite anglers' resort. There is some decent pike fishing above the weir.

The salmon rarely get above this point, except in the spawning season. From this point to Wheldrake Bridge the fishing rights on the right side have been purchased by Messrs. Aspinall & Masterman, fish and game dealers, Coney Street, York. They also rent the remainder of the fishing in the Derwent on both sides from Sutton to Ellerton from the respective owners, with the exception of one short length opposite Thorganby. Permission for fishing their length of the river must be had from Messrs. Aspinall & Masterman. They reserve the salmon fishing entirely to themselves, but occasionally grant leave for the coarse fishing. The fishing below Wheldrake Bridge is fairly good. At East Cottingwith it has fallen off somewhat, through the indiscriminate netting of the becks and backwashes by the village loafers. At Cottingwith Ferry the Pocklington Canal enters. This canal, which is nine miles long, is the property of the North Eastern Railway Company, but is rented for fishing purposes by the York Angling Club, from whose secretary day tickets may be procured. The pike fishing in the canal is very good. The principal coarse fish in the river about here are pike, roach, chub, and bream.

Wheldrake Bridge is two and three-quarter miles below Sutton Weir. Storthwaite is a mile and a quarter wide of the bridge. Thicket Park commences half-a-mile below Wheldrake Bridge, and ends at Ferry House Inn, three-quarters of a mile below on the right bank. The ferry is just below the inn. On the opposite side, the Pocklington Canal joins the river. West Cottingwith stands on the right side of the river, and East Cottingwith on the left. There are inns at both places. The nearest railway station is Bubwith. Thorganby, where there is an inn, is about a mile below Cottingwith Ferry. It is at Thorganby, on the left side, where the above mentioned short length—about a quarter of a mile—of private fishing comes in. Ellerton Landing is three-quarters of a mile below Thorganby. Ellerton is half-a-mile wide of the river. There is an inn, Bubwith being the nearest railway station.

Ellerton Landing is the end of Messrs. Aspinall & Masterman's fishing. From this point to the confluence with the Ouse, the fishing is practically free so long as anglers conduct themselves like sportsmen, and keep out of the meadows when the crops are on. This applies to both sides, except where private grounds intervene. There is a fair quantity of all kinds of coarse fish—chub, dace, and eels predominating. Also some very decent pike. Menthorpe is a fishing centre much frequented at the week-end by the Leeds angler, Sunday fishing being allowed. The best length is from Menthorpe to Bubwith. Mr. E. Howden, Half Moon Inn, Menthorpe Ferry, is glad to afford the angler any information.

Aughton, where there is an inn, is a mile and a half below Ellerton Landing. Bubwith Bridge is a mile and a quarter below Aughton Landing. North Duffield stands on the opposite side to Bubwith. There is an inn. Menthorpe Ferry and inn are a mile below Bubwith Bridge. It is three-quarters of a mile from the ferry to Menthorpe Station. Breighton is half-a-mile below the ferry. Bubwith is the nearest station. Wressel, where there is a railway station, is a mile and three-quarters below Breighton. At Wressel the Hull and Selby Railway crosses the river. Loftsome Bridge is three-quarters of a mile below Wressel. Barmby is two and a quarter miles below Loftsome Bridge. At Barmby there are inns and a ferry, and half-a-mile below the Derwent enters the River Ouse, opposite Long Drax. There is a ferry at this place across the Ouse. Wressel is the nearest railway station. The total length of the Derwent from source to mouth is seventy-seven miles.

RIVER DOE OR DALE BECK.

The River Doe or Dale Beck rises on Blea Moor on Ingleton Fells on the slopes of Ingleborough 1,400ft. above the sea. Here it is called Little Dale Beck, and it receives above Winterscales a great number of small moorland streams. These are the only tributaries of importance. Its chief gathering grounds are the south-east side of Whernside and the north-west side of Ingleborough. About four and a half miles from its source, through a fault in the limestone strata, the Dale Beck enters the ground at Long Slack and runs underground for about a quarter of mile, whence it issues at Philpin, a quarter of a mile below which place it re-enters the ground at Weathercote Cave, re-issuing immediately below at Jingle Pot. Jingle Pot is 848 feet above sea level. There is no fishing above that place. From Jingle Pot to Dale House on the left and on the right to about half a mile above Dale House the fishing is in private hands. Below those places the fishing on both sides of the stream is in the hands of the Ingleton Angling Association the whole way to the junction with the Kingsdale Beck. The whole of the association water (all trout) is fishable by ticket, procurable from the hon. sec. Mr. Samuel Worthington, Ingleton, or at the Wheat Sheaf, Ingleton. This ticket also embraces fishing in the Greta and Kingsdale Becks, for details refer to those streams. Ingleton, where there is good accommodation and a railway station, is the best centre. God's Bridge is a mile below Jingle Pot, and Dale House is two miles below the same place. Twistleton Manor comes in about a mile and a half below Dale House. Ingleton Bridge is four and a half miles below Jingle Pot. There is a weir just above the bridge and immediately below the Doe joins the Kingsdale Beck in forming the River Greta.

RIVER DON.

The River Don has its source 1350 feet above sea level at Grains Moss, on the Austonley and Penistone Moors, south-east of Holme Moss. It is formed about three-quarters of a mile inside the county boundary by the conjuction of the Great Grains and

Black Grough, two small moorland streams. The Dunfordbridge Reservoirs, belonging to the Dewsbury Corporation, are formed at the top end of the valley through which the infant river runs and receives these moorland streams. The original stream leaves the lower reservoir at Dunfordbridge, which is only two miles from the source. Thence it flows to Penistone, and below to Sheffield, through what was once one of the loveliest valleys in England. Here the river is bounded by Wharncliffe Woods, made famous by Sir Walter Scott in "Ivanhoe." Below Sheffield it flows through a broad vale to Conisborough and Doncaster. Below Doncaster the river becomes a deep sluggish stream, with steep sloping banks running through the flat country bordering on Hatfield Chase, by Thorne, to Goole. This is the country which at one time was all under water, and was reclaimed by a system of drainage by Cornelius Vermuyden and his Dutch settlers. Originally the Don ran from New Bridge, about four miles below Thorne, due north, and emptied itseif into the Aire, about a mile above Rawcliffe. This old river course is now filled up, with the exception of one stretch of dead water at Turnbridge, which contains a fair quantity of eels, and Vermuyden and his settlers constructed the present river course, a huge canal which runs from New Bridge to Goole, thus getting the outlet to a much lower level and draining the water off the whole country. The Don enters the Ouse between Goole and Old Goole. The river is tidal, and the spring tides flow to the breakwater at Long Sandall Bridge. The salmon do not get any higher up the river than this breakwater. The river is navigable from Goole to Aldwark below Rotherham, and also forwards to Sheffield by the aid of a canal. The Manchester, Sheffield, and Lincolnshire Railway runs parallel with the river from Dunfordbridge to Sheffield, the Sheffield and Rotherham Railway to Rotherham, the Midland Railway from Rotherham to Swinton, and from Swinton the South Yorkshire, Doncaster, and Goole Railway.

This once beautiful angling stream is now very highly polluted for the greater part of its course, and for a distance of forty-five miles is absolutely unfishable. The principal tributaries are the Little Don River (see *post*), the Moor Hall Beck (a good trout stream, but strictly private), the Ewden Beck (another excellent trout stream, also private), the River Loxley (polluted, see *post*), the River Rother (polluted the whole of its course through Yorkshire, see *post*), the River Dearn (see *ante*), the Bentley and Arksey Drain (an angling stream), and the River Went (see *post*). The Dunfordbridge Reservoirs are well stocked with trout. Colonel Stanhope, of Canon Hall, Barnsley, who has the sporting rights, has a fish-breeding establishment, and turns large quantities of fish in yearly. The fishing, however, is private. The fishing in the river from Dunfordbridge to Hazlehead, three miles, is in the hands of Colonel Stanhope, on the right bank, and Charles Chatman, Esq., Carlcoates Hall, on the left. This is also private. Nothing but trout. The fishing is no good below Hazelhead. About a mile below the place the ochre water from the Bullhouse Mines enters the river, and here the pollutions commence, and gradually increase from various sources all the way down until the culminating point is reached below Rotherham. Sheffield and Rotherham are the chief offenders, and here the river becomes a solid, inky mass of pollution. Although there are plenty of clear water tributaries below, the sediment does not settle nor the river clear until past Doncaster, and the Don from Hazelhead to Doncaster is unfishable. Penistone is three miles and three-quarters below Hazlehead. The Little Don (also polluted in its lower reaches) enters eight miles below Penistone. The Ewden Beck enters a mile and three-quarters below the Little Don. The River Loxley enters six miles below the Ewden Beck. The centre of Sheffield is a mile and a half below the River Loxley. The River Rother enters at Rotherham, seven and a quarter miles below Sheffield. Aldwark is two and a half miles below Rotherham. Mexborough is six miles below Aldwark. Two miles below Mexborough the River Dearn enters. Half-a-mile below Dearn Mouth is Conisborough. Doncaster is six miles below Conisborough.

Below Doncaster, fish gradually begin to put in an appearance again, although the angling is very little good above Wheatley. In the length of the river from Doncaster to Goole there is nothing but coarse fish, except the salmon, which are only found below Long Sandall. The salmon fishing generally has fallen off a great deal. It suffers from the flushes of refuse brought down in the freshes from above, therefore the supply varies. Bream, pike, chub, roach, and eels are found, and flounders in the lower reaches. The eel fishing is very good, and the professional fishermen from Goole devote their attention to that principally. They row up the river and settle eel-heaps at various places, and collect them in returning. Good catches are often made. No nets are allowed. The salmon fishing is strictly private. It is difficult to fish the river below Barnby Dun without the aid of a boat, particularly at low tide, on account of the deep mud-banks. The whole of the coarse fishing from Doncaster to Goole is practically open. Mile Thorn Ferry is a mile and a half below Doncaster. There is also a lock and weir at this place. Wheatley Hall is a mile below the weir. Arksey Landing is three-quarters of a mile below Wheatley Hall. It is one mile from the landing to Arksey. Long Sandall Bridge and breakwater are half-a-mile below the landing. The spring tides flow to this point. There is an inn at Long Sandall. Kirk Sandall is a mile and a half below Long Sandall Bridge. The Bentley and Arksey Drain, which holds fish, enters here. A mile below Kirk Sandall is Barnby Dun Turn Bridge. There are inns and a railway station at Barnby Dun. A mile and a quarter below Barnby Dun is Wilsick Ferry. Thorp Marsh Drain enters here. A mile and a quarter below Wilsick Ferry is Bramwith Ferry. The ordinary tides flow to this point. The Warncarr and Braithwaite Drain enters at Kirk Bramwith. A mile and three-quarters below Bramwith is Stainforth Bridge. There are inns, a lock, and a railway station at Stainforth. A mile and a quarter below Stainforth is Fishlake Ferry. There are inns at Fishlake. Thorne Quay is a mile and a quarter below Fishlake. There are several inns and two railway stations at Thorne. A mile and a half below Thorne Quay the Jubilee Bridge crosses the river. A mile and a half below Jubilee Bridge the River Went enters (see *post*). Soak Dyke enters immediately below. A mile below Went Mouth is New Bridge. There is an inn at New Bridge. Rawcliffe is the nearest railway station, two miles. From this point the river does not follow the old course of the Don, but enters the great cut made by the Dutch settlers, and is called from here to Goole "Dutch

River." Greenland Drain enters three-quarters of a mile below New Bridge. Three-quarters of a mile below Greenland Drain Black Drain enters, and Thorn Tree Drain a quarter of a mile still lower. A quarter of a mile below Thorn Tree Drain is Rawcliffe Bridge. It is one mile to Rawcliffe Station. There are several inns at Rawcliffe. Rawcliffe Bridge Drain enters just below the bridge. New Drain and Dobeller Drain enter a quarter of a mile below, and Pasture Drain a quarter of a mile still lower. Airmyn Pasture Drain enters a mile below Rawcliffe Bridge, and the Decoy Drain and Old Drain immediately below. Half-a-mile below Airmyn Pasture Drain is Oaks Hill and Beverley's Bridge. Immediately above the bridge Towns Drain enters, and immediately below New Potter Grange Drain. Smith's Bridge is half-a-mile below Oaks Hill Bridge. Below the bridge a drain enters on the left, and a quarter of a mile lower down Swang Drain enters. Three-quarters of a mile below Smith's Bridge is Goole Bridge. A quarter of a mile below the bridge the River Don or Dutch River enters the Ouse. Goole stands on the left bank, and Old Goole on the right. The total length of the River Don is seventy-three and a quarter miles.

LITTLE DON RIVER.

The Little Don River has its source on the Langsett Moors, a few miles south of the source of the main Don. It is formed by the confluence of the Loftshaw and Laund Clough Brooks, which drain the Cloudberry and Harden Moors. The top reaches run through wild moorlands, below which, the river runs down a valley, closed in by high hills, until it enters the main Don at Deepcar. From Langsett to the river mouth the Langsett and Sheffield highway runs parallel with the stream. The lower half of the river is polluted, but the top half is a beautiful trout stream, and holds some nice fish. The fishing in this part of the river, however, is all private, but permission in some cases is occasionally granted by the owners or tenants. From the source to about a mile below Midhope Bridge, a distance of five miles, is the fishable part of the river. The tributaries are neither numerous nor important.

Langsett is three miles below the source. Here there is an inn, and it is two miles to Hazlewood Bridge Station. Midhope Bridge is a mile below Langsett, and a mile below Midhope Bridge the ochre water from some disused mines flows into the river, which is polluted from this point, these pollutions being still further increased by the refuse from some chemical works lower down. Midhopestones Bridge is a mile and a half below Midhope Bridge. A mile and a half below Midhopestones is Onsliven Bridge, and Stocksbridge is a mile and a half still lower. A mile and a quarter below Stocksbridge is Deepcar Bridge, and just below here the stream enters the main Don, opposite Wharncliffe Woods. The total length of the river is ten miles.

RIVER DOVE (DEARN).

The River Dove was originally formed by the Rockley Dyke and Rough Green Brook, which are now the principal feeders of the Worsborough Reservoir, which feeds the Worsborough branch of the Dearn and Dove Canal, and runs down Worsborough Dale to Nether Woodhall. There is good fishing both in the canal and reservoir. The canal is about two miles in length, and is practically open fishing. The farmers do not interfere so long as anglers conduct themselves properly. Permission to fish the reservoir can be had from Mr. Mann. Day tickets can be had at 6d. each from the reservoir keeper. A charge of 5s. a day is made for the use of the boat. Pike, chub, roach, eels, and bream. Nearest railway station Elsecar.

RIVER DOVE (RYEDALE).

The River Dove rises at Middlehead, on Farndale Moors, above Kirkbymoorside, 1,300 feet above the sea. In its higher reaches it flows through the moors for a few miles. From Yoadwath Sinks to Spring Head, near Bog Hall, the river enters the openings in the limestone rock and runs underground for about a mile, except in flood time, when the ordinary bed of the river is full, and the fish can get up stream. Above Lowna Bridge it is good moorland fishing for about six miles, there being a plentiful supply of trout. Below Lowna Bridge the river enters some lovely glens, and is thickly bordered with trees. A short two-length rod is needed to fish this part of the stream to Yoadwath, above which point there is nothing but trout fishing, which is very good. Above Keldholme the river rushes out of the rock in a volume. Below this point the larger fish, both trout and grayling, are found, and below Kirkby Mills, where the deeps commence, the best of the fishing is grayling, with a few chub and dace, and an occasional pike. The principal tributary is the Hodge Beck—also a capital angling stream. The best centres are Kirkbymoorside and Helmsley, at both of which places there are railway stations and very good inns. The Dove enters the River Rye at Salton. The trout fishing is first-class early in the season. The same can be said of the grayling fishing later on. The stream is fishable on the left side from the source to Gillamoor Bridge by ticket, procurable from the Earl of Feversham's agent, and below Gillamoor Bridge to the confluence with the Rye permission can be had from the owners and tenants. On the right side from the source to Yoadwath Mill (then comes a break), and from Kirkby Mills to Hodge Beck also fishable by ticket as above. The break, and below Hodge Beck to the Rye, can be fished by permission from the tenants. The above-mentioned tickets are procurable at the Feversham Estate Offices, Helmsley, *viâ* York, at the following rates: season, which ends October 1st, 12s.; three months, 7s.; one month, 3s.; one week, 1s. These tickets also allow the angler to fish in the Riccall and Hodge (see *post*). Artificial fly or minnow only. No worm fishing on any pretence. Close time for trout, October 1st to March 31st. No fish to be taken under 6½in. All baskets and tickets open to the inspection of Lord Feversham's keepers, who are not allowed to receive gratuities.

Lowna or Gillamoor Bridge is ten and a half miles below the source. The Earl of Feversham's water, which is fishable by ticket, ends here on the left side. From this point to the Rye permission to fish can easily be obtained from the tenants so long as anglers conduct themselves like sportsmen. The same restrictions are in force on the whole of the river. Gillamoor is half-a-mile below the bridge. The nearest railway station is Kirkbymoorside. Hutton-le-Hole, where there is an inn, is three-quarters of a mile below Gilamoor and three-quarters of a mile wide of the stream. Yoadwath Mill is three and a quarter miles below Gillamoor. This is the end of the first length of Lord Feversham's water on the right side. Below to Kirkby Mills permission can be had from the tenants. The above restrictions also apply to this water. Yoadwath Sinks are just below. Here the river sinks into the ground and reappears at Spring Head, which is a mile below the sinks. Keldholme is a quarter of a mile below Spring Head, and Kirkby Mills another quarter below Keldholme. Kirkby Mills is half-a-mile from Kirkbymoorside. There are several inns and a railway station. Here Lord Feversham's water, fishable by ticket, recommences on the right side, and extends to Hodge Beck. Edston, where there is an inn, is a mile and three-quarters below Kirkby Mills. The Hodge Beck enters just below.

This is the principal tributary of the Dove, and likewise an important angling stream. Below here to the Rye permission to fish can be had from the tenants. Salton Bridge is a mile below Hodge Beck. There is an inn at Salton, and the nearest railway station is Slingsby, four miles. The River Dove enters the Rye about three-quarters of a mile below Salton Bridge. The total length of the river is twenty-two and three-quarter miles.

DRIFFIELD STREAM.

The Driffield Stream has its origin at the Keld, at King's Mills, which lies between Great and Little Driffield. Through a fault in the limestone rock it runs, for a considerable distance, underground, until it makes its appearance in one volume at the Keld. Just below its source it receives a short stream which is formed by the confluence of the Emswell and Little Driffield Becks, and these, along with the Kirkburn Beck, are the principal tributaries. The stream is very irregular in its course, running almost parallel with the Driffield Canal to about half-a-mile below Wansford. The whole of the stream to the junction with the navigation (about ten miles) is now known as the Driffield Stream, though, in reality, the River Hull commences at the foot of the mill race, three and a half miles below the Keld, and is a continuation of the Driffield Beck. It is a gentle running stream, overgrown with short weeds in many parts, but it is one of the very best trout streams in Yorkshire, the fish averaging about 1lb. The water, however, is very exclusive, and is strictly preserved by a club of twenty members. Entrance fee £10 10s.; annual subscription £10 10s., which includes six day tickets for friends. The riparian owners are also entitled to silver transferable tickets. All fish under 11in. to be returned. Artificial fly only. Season commences first Tuesday after April 20th, and ends October 1st. Limited to ten brace a day. Hon. secretary, Colonel Brooksbank, Middleton-on-the-Wold; beck watcher, Cass, Bell Mills, Driffield. The club length extends from the Keld to a little below Skerne Beck, about a mile and a half below Wansford, the total length of the water being about seven miles and three-quarters, following the windings of the stream. Driffield, where there is a railway station, is about a quarter of a mile from the Keld. Kirkburn Beck enters a little below, and a little above Bell Mills. Wansford is five miles below the Keld and Skerne Beck is a mile and a quarter below Wansford. From Corps Landing, which is just below Skerne Beck, the fishing is practically open until the stream runs into the navigation at Emmotland Bridge, which is about two miles below.

DRIFFIELD NAVIGATION.

Driffield Navigation, which holds some big fish, runs over portions of the River Hull and Frodingham Beck. It commences at the Driffleld Basin, which is on the south side of Driffield, and whose chief feeder is Etherington Thorns Waterfall Howl, which runs through the town of Driffield to the basin. The canal runs parallel with Driffield Beck to considerably below Wansford Bridge. Nafferton Beck, one of the chief feeders, runs in at Wansford. From the lock below Wansford Bridge the canal takes a straight course across country until it joins Frodingham Beck below Brigham. It now follows the course of Frodingham Beck, which has been made navigable, until it enters the River Hull at the point where the Driffield trout stream ends. The navigable portion of Frodingham Beck is known as part of the Driffield Navigation. The whole of the fishing, which is very good in this navigation, is free. Trout which average 1lb., pike, roach, perch, and other coarse fish. The water is much used by Hull Angling Clubs to fish their matches. The best length is from Brigham Beck end to Snakeholme Lock. Close time for trout, October 15th to March 15th, both inclusive. There is a railway station and inns at Driffield. Whin Hill Lock is a mile and three-quarters below Driffield, and Wansford Bridge is a mile below Whin Hill. Snakeholme Lock is half-a-mile below Wansford. There are inns at Wansford. A mile below the lock is Brigham Bridge, and three-quarters of a mile below that bridge the navigation joins Frodingham Beck. The length of navigation over Frodingham Beck before it joins the River Hull is three-quarters of a mile. The nearest railway station from the junction is Cranswick, three miles. The Driffield Navigation runs over what was originally the River Hull for about a mile and a quarter to Struncheonhill Lock. The total length of the navigation is about seven miles. The Yorkshire Fishery Board have turned one thousand yearling trout into the canal at the commencement of the present season.

RIVER ESK.

The River Esk rises on Westerdale Moor, 1,250 feet above the sea level, at Esklets, a number of small streamlets at the head of a deep moorland valley, and flows into the sea at Whitby. The bed of the river is chiefly limestone rock, which makes it bad feeding ground except in flood-time. The principal tributaries and breeding becks are the following, which enter the river in the order named: Basedale Beck, Commondale and Sleddale Becks, Danby Beck, Clither Beck, Little Fryup Beck, Great Fryup Beck, Stonegate Beck, Churchdale Beck, Glaisdale Beck, Butter Beck, the Murk Esk (the principal tributary), and Iburndale Beck. The tide flows ordinarily to the weir at Ruswarp, but the spring tides reach Briggswath. The Whitby and Cleveland Railway lies contiguous with the river from Whitby to Castleton, where it branches off into Commondale. The Whitby and Pickering Railway branches off at Grosmont. The whole of the fishing is high-class. Salmon, sea trout, and brown trout. The best salmon length is that of the Esk Fisheries Association, and the best for trout the Lealholm and Danby Club length. Trout run small above Westerdale.

From the source to Westerdale Bridge the fish run somewhat small. Permission must be had from the tenants. Westerdale is four and three-quarter miles below the source. There is an inn, and Castleton is the nearest railway station. Below Westerdale to Commondale Beck there is some fair trout fishing in the hands of the landlords and tenants. Commondale Beck, which receives Sleddale Beck, enters the Esk on the left, two miles and a quarter below Westerdale. The fishing in the lower length of this beck is good, and is free so long as anglers do not misconduct themselves. From Commondale Beck the fishing is free to Danby Beck, both sides, subject to the above stipulation. Salmon are sometimes caught as high up as this. The fishing for salmon is from February 2nd to November 1st, and for trout March 16th to September 30th, all dates inclusive. Castleton Bridge is a quarter of a mile below Commondale Beck. Here there is an inn and railway station.

Danby Beck is three-quarters of a mile below Castleton Bridge. From Danby Beck to Duck Bridge (two and a half miles) the fishing is private on both sides. Ainthorpe Bridge is a mile and a quarter below Danby Beck. Ainthorpe stands on the right bank and Dale end on the left. There is a railway station at the latter place and inns at both villages. Danby Castle is a quarter of a mile wide of Duck Bridge.

From Duck Bridge to the wash below Lealholm Bridge, the fishing on both sides belongs to the Lealholm and Danby Anglers' Club. Patron, Viscount Downe ; president, W. Wood, Esq. ; hon. secretary, Mr. George Readman, Lealholm, Grosmont, *viâ* York. Annual subscription, 21s. ; limited to twenty members. A limited number of monthly and day tickets at 10s. 6d. and 3s. respectively. No member allowed to fish more than twenty-one days each year. Only one rod allowed. Lures : artificial fly, natural or artificial minnow, and worm on and after June 1st. Limit for trout, 7in. Close time, salmon, November 2nd to February 1st; trout, October 1st to March 31st. Dogs prohibited. Keepers have power to examine baskets and tickets. Lealholm Bridge is four and a quarter miles below Duck Bridge. From Lealholm Bridge to Beggars' Bridge, Glaisdale, three and three-quarter miles, the fishing is private on both sides. Glaisdale Station is near Beggars' Bridge. Glaisdale village is half-a-mile wide of the river. There is an inn.

The Esk Fishery Association extends, both sides, from Beggars' Bridge to Sleights Bridge, nine miles. Chairman, J. H. Keighley, Esq.; vice-chairman, H. A. H. Rastall, Esq.; hon. secretary, R. B. L. Johnston, Esq.; clerk, to whom applications must be made, Mr. William Brown, 8, Baxtergate, Whitby; watchers, Wm. Luke, Flowergate, Whitby; and Hy. Brocket, Glaisdale. Limited to fifty members, in addition to which fifteen visitors' tickets are issued. The visitors' tickets are availabe for twenty-eight days from date of issue, price, £2 2s. A deposit of 10s. must be paid upon the issuing of a ticket, to be returned only if the ticket be surrendered on or before the evening of the day on which it expires. Application for these tickets to be made to the clerk in writing. Visitors' tickets not available after September 30th. A visitor for the purposes of the club shall be one who resides for at least fourteen days within four miles of Whitby Bridge or of any water rented by the Esk Fishery Association. Subscription, 42s. the season. Entrance fee, 42s. No short period tickets. One rod only. Lures: artificial fly and worm, and artificial or dead minnow. Before July 1st, artificial fly only. No worm or minnow fishing for trout allowed on the Egton Estate. Limit for trout, 8in. No Sunday fishing. Watchers have power to examine panniers, &c. Members can lend their tickets to friends actually stopping at their houses. The licenses for this district are: salmon, season, 10s.; month, 5s.; day, 2s. 6d. Day and month licenses do not avail after June 30th. Trout license, season, 1s. 6d. Salmon licenses may be had from the clerk; F. W. Howe, "Gazette" Office, Whitby; W. Bradley, Fox and Hounds Inn, Ainthorpe; and the above-mentioned water bailiffs,

Luke and Brocket. Trout licenses may also be had from the above, and likewise from J. Cooke, Ainthorpe ; Sedman, Ruswarp ; Elwick, Grosmont ; Stanforth, Beck Hole ; Hill, Goathland ; Medd, Post Office, Castleton. Egton Bridge is two miles below Beggars' Bridge. Here there is a railway station and a good inn. Grosmont Bridge is two miles below Egton Bridge. At Grosmont there are inns and a railway station. This is the junction for Malton and York. Five miles below Grosmont Bridge is Sleights Bridge. Here there is a railway station. Briggswath stands on the left of Sleights Bridge, and the spring tides flow to this point. Sleights village is three-quarters of a mile wide of the river. There is an inn near the station. From Sleights Bridge to the sea the fishing belongs to the lord of the manor, Sir Charles Strickland, Bart., who reserves Ruswarp Dam, that is from Sleights Bridge to Ruswarp Weir, for himself and friends. This water is also fishable by ticket, procurable from Sir Charles's water bailiff, William Sedman, Ruswarp. From Sleights Bridge to Ruswarp Weir it is a mile and a half. At Ruswarp there are inns and a railway station. From here to the sea, two miles and a quarter, the fishing is free on sufferance, except the salmon fishing, which is reserved by the lord of the manor. Small boats can come up from Whitby as far as Ruswarp Dam, from which good fishing can be had. Whitby is the best centre for the angler, as there is a good service of trains through the dale to all the best lengths of water.

RIVER FOSS.

The River Foss has its source 540 feet above sea level, at the corner of Yearsley Moor, near the south-east corner of Newburgh Park, and about three-quarters of a mile north-west of the village of Yearsley. About half a mile down its course it enters the Foss Navigation Reservoir, which was constructed on the original course of the river as a service reservoir at the time that the Foss was navigable. Formerly the river was navigable from Sheriff Hutton Bridge to the Ouse at York, part of the way by the aid of a canal which ran from Sheriff Hutton Bridge to Double Rise Bridge. For the purposes of navigation the river has long since fallen into disuse, and the head of the canal has been partly filled up. This is now known as River Head, and the river itself, which enters thirteen miles below its source, is more generally known at this point as Sheriff Hutton Beck. It is, in fact, nothing but a mere beck in the first thirteen miles, without any tributaries below the Foss Navigation Reservoir, which receives Heron Gill Beck, which runs from the fish ponds in Newburgh Park. This beck part of the Foss holds fish, trout and chub, which run somewhat small, and the fishing is in the hands of the owners and tenants, from whom permission must be obtained. From Double Rise Bridge the river is much more pretentious. It runs past Strensall and Huntington to York, and this is undoubtedly the best part of the fishing. The chub, roach, dace, and eel fishing is very good, and pike are found up to fourteen and fifteen pounds weight.

The nearest stations to the source are Coxwold, three and a half miles, and Gilling, two and a half miles. Mill Green Bridge is three miles below the source, from which bridge it is three-quarters of a mile to Crayke. Three and three-quarter miles below Mill Green Bridge is Stillington Bridge. At Stillington there are inns, and it is five miles to Tollerton Station. Two miles below Stillington Bridge is Foss Bridge, from which it is a mile and three-quarters to Sutton on the one hand, and a mile and a quarter to Farlington on the other. Inns at both places, Flaxton nearest railway station. Two miles below Foss Bridge is Sheriff Hutton Bridge. The canal was formerly fed from this point. The canal is grown up with rushes, and is no use for angling purposes. This also applies to certain parts of the river below, which are only fishable before vegetation starts in spring, and after it is dead in autumn. From the bridge it is two and a half miles to Strensall Station, and one and three-quarters to Sheriff Hutton. From Sheriff Hutton Bridge the towing path runs down the right side of the river: Double Rise Bridge is two miles below. From this point on the right to Towthorpe Bridge (three miles), permission to fish can be had from the tenants, and on the left to Strensall Lock (one mile), permission must be had from the Government officials, York Barracks. Strensall Bridge is just below Strensall Lock, and the railway station is adjoining. From Strensall Lock on the left, the whole way to the Ouse, permission to fish can be had from the owners and tenants. On the right from Towthorpe Bridge to Haxby Bridge (one mile), the fishing is private. From Haxby Bridge to opposite Earswick (half-a-mile), leave can be had from Haxby Lock keeper. Railway station and inn at Haxby. From opposite Earswick to Huntington Bridge (one mile) on the right the fishing is private, and from Huntington Bridge to York it is all open fishing. There are inns at Huntington. Dowker Bridge is a quarter of a mile below Huntington Bridge, and Swing Bridge half-a-mile still lower. York and Market Weighton Railway crosses a quarter of a mile below Swing Bridge, and Yearsley Bridge and Lock are a mile lower down. The river enters York at Monk Bridge, a mile below Yearsley Bridge. Foss Bridge and Castle Bridge being three-quarters of a mile and a mile lower respectively. Blue Bridge is a quarter of a mile below Castle Bridge, and at this point the Foss enters the river Ouse on the low side of York. The total length of the river is twenty-three and a quarter miles. The Amalgamated Anglers' Association are at the present time negotiating with the York Corporation for a portion of the lower Foss for the purpose of preserving the same.

RIVER GRETA (LUNESDALE).

The River Greta commences at Ingleton, at the junction of the Kingsdale Beck (see *post*) and the Doe or Dale Beck (see *ante*), 370 feet above the sea. These streams are its principal tributaries, the only other being the Aspland Beck. The river, after passing through a charming country, enters the River Lune on the low side of Tunstall, and two and a half miles outside the Yorkshire boundary. The fishing is first-class Salmon do not get above Burton Weir. There is nothing but trout above that point. From the source to Burton Bridge, on both sides of the river, the fishing is in the hands of the Ingleton Angling Association, whose waters are fishable by ticket, procurable from Mr. Samuel Worthington, hon. secretary, Ingleton, or at the Wheat Sheaf. For particulars see Kingsdale Beck. Below Burton Bridge the fishing on both sides is in the hands of the owners and tenants, from whom permission must be had. Ingleton is the best centre. There is good accommodation and railway service. Greet Bridge is half-a-mile below Ingleton Bridge. Here the highway crosses from Kirkby Lonsdale to Clapham. A mile and a half below Greet Bridge Aspland Beck enters. Half-a-mile below Aspland Beck is Limeholme Green Bridge. A mile below Limeholme Green Bridge is Burton-in-Lonsdale. Here the Ingleton Angling Association water ends. This association also have water on the River Doe and Kingsdale Beck. There are inns at Burton. It is a mile and three-quarters to Lower Bentham, and two miles and three-quarters to High Bentham Railway Station. At Burton-in-Lonsdale the weir is just below the bridge. A mile and a quarter below Burton Bridge the river leaves the county of York on the right, and ditto a quarter of a mile lower down on the left. The total length of the river is about seven and a half miles.

RIVER GRETA (TEESDALE).

The River Greta, immortalised by Sir Walter Scott, and Turner the artist, is an important angling tributary of the Tees. The lower part of the river is very picturesque, particularly about Rokeby and Brignall. The Greta rises on the county boundary near Rey Cross, an old British camp on Broad Moss, on Stainmoor and 1,350 feet above sea level. In the first mile and three-quarters of its course it gathers numerous small moorland streams when its first principal tributary, Ay Gill Beck enters. The South Durham and Lancashire Union Railway runs parallel with the river from its source to Bowes. From the source to God's Bridge permission to fish can be had from the various owners and tenants on both sides. There is a waterfall three and a half miles below the source. God's Bridge, or Mellwaters Bridge, is two miles below this waterfall. From God's Bridge to Trough Beck, on the right bank, tickets to fish (5s. the season) can be had from Mr. Dent, Mellwaters, Bowes, Darlington. Below Trough Beck, on the same side as the Tees, the fishing is private. On the left bank, from God's Bridge to Rutherford Bridge, permission can be had from the tenants. Below Rutherford Bridge to the Tees, on the left side, the fishing in private. Mellwaters is just below God's Bridge. Trough Beck is a mile and a quarter below God's Bridge. A mile and a half below Trough Beck is Bowes. Here there are inns and a railway station. Rutherford Bridge is three miles below Bowes. A mile and a quarter below this Bridge is Brignall Mill. Brignall is two and a half miles below the mill. Greta Bridge, where there is an inn, is a mile lower down. Here the Great North Road crosses the river, along which road it is thirteen miles to Catterick Bridge Station. The nearest railway station is Barnard Castle, four miles. Rokeby Park runs from the bridge along the left bank. Mortham Tower and Rokeby Hall, on opposite banks, are a mile below the bridge. Dairy Bridge is just below, and immediately afterwards the Greta enters the Tees. The trout fishing is excellent throughout. The total length of the River Greta is seventeen and a half miles.

HAYBURN WIKE.

Hayburn Wike is formed by the junction of two rapid little streams, namely, Hayburn Beck—which is a continuation of Thorny Beck—and Staintondale Beck, both of which run from Staintondale Moors. Thorny Beck rises at Pye Rigg, 675 feet above sea level, and runs south to the highway and east to Hayburn Bridge, distance two and a quarter miles. Below Hayburn Bridge the stream is called Hayburn Beck for three-quarters of a mile, when it is joined by Staintondale Beck and becomes Hayburn Wike, emptying itself into the sea a short half-mile below. Staintondale Beck rises at Brown Rigg, on Staintondale Moor, about a quarter of a mile east of Thorny Beck Head, running down the dale for two and a quarter miles until it joins the other stream. These streams are full of little trout. It is only possible to fish them "up stream worm," as the dales through which they run are so heavily wooded. Leave to fish the lower part of the water is granted by the landlord of the hotel at Hayburn Wike Station, which is within three minutes walk of the junction of the streams. The farmers readily grant leave to fish the remainder of the water. Hayburn Wike enters the sea six miles north of Scarborough. The Whitby and Scarborough Railway runs through the place.

RIVER HODDER.

The River Hodder, which is the principal angling tributary of the Ribble, rises 1,430 feet above the sea, on the Yorkshire county boundary, between Croasdale Fells, Hill Fell, and Lamb Fell, and its higher reaches run through a very hilly and irregular country above Slaidburn, from which numerous small tributaries fall to the main stream. The principal tributaries on the river are Bridge House Beck, Dunsop River, Langden Brook, and the River Loud. Dunsop River enters the Hodder at Thornyholme. It is formed by the Brennand and Whitendale Rivers, which run from Brennand and Whitendale Fells respectively, and drain the country known as the Forest of Bowland. The Langden River enters the Hodder about half-a-mile below Thornyholme, and runs from the north-east side of Bleasdale Moors, receiving several mountain streams in its course. The River Loud runs from the south side of Parlick, and drains the country between Chipping and Longridge Fell. The smaller tributaries that run to the Hodder in its course are very numerous, and fall from Easington Fell, Standridge Hill, Browsholme Moor, and the east end of Longridge Fell. It is entirely a Yorkshire stream until it reaches Burholme, just below which it touches the county of Lancaster on one side, and for the remainder of its course forms the boundary between that county and the county of York. In its lower reaches it is very picturesque, and is one of the best all-round fishing streams in England. Spring for brown trout, July, August, and September for sea trout, and September and October for salmon. Most of the tributaries are in private hands. On the highest reaches of the river the fish run very small, and what fishing there is which is worth anything above Slaidburn is in private hands. The river watchers are John Wrigley, West Bradford, near Clitheroe; and Robert Moon, Cross Street, Clitheroe. Close time for trout, October 1st; salmon, November 1st.

Lock Bridge is three miles from the source. Chapel House Bridge is one and three-quarter miles below Lock Bridge. There is a weir a quarter of a mile below the bridge. Stocks in Bowland is half a mile below the bridge. Grange Mill Bridge is a quarter of a mile lower down. Bridge House Beck enters below the bridge. Two and a quarter miles below Grange Mill Bridge is Holmshead Bridge. Barn Gill Beck enters just above. Slaidburn Bridge is half-a-mile below Holmshead Bridge. The fishing above this point is private. Croasdale Brook enters at Slaidburn Bridge. From the bridge it is seven miles to Chatburn, the nearest railway station. From Slaidburn Bridge to Dunmow (one mile) the fishing is private on both sides. From Dunmow to Heading (two and a half miles) fishing on both sides can be had by staying at the Parker's Arms, Newton. Two days fishing only can be had. They are very particular not to exceed this. Newton Bridge is a mile below Dunmow. Easington Brook enters above the bridge. Birkett Brook enters opposite Heaning. From Heaning, on the right to Dunsop Bridge, and on the left to Burholme Bridge, the fishing is private. Rough Sike Beck enters a mile below Heaning, and Dunsop Bridge is a mile and three-quarters below the beck. Dunsop River enters at the bridge, and Langden Brook half-a-mile below. Burholme Bridge is a mile below Dunsop Bridge. Just below Burholme Bridge the right side of the Hodder enters the county of Lancaster. From Dunsop Bridge on the Lancashire side, and from Burholme Bridge on the Yorkshire side to Doeford Bridge, tickets to fish can be had free from Mr. W. Cowgill, Whitewell Hotel. This is a first-class hotel offering the best accommodation to sportsmen and tourists, and stands in one of the prettiest valleys in the country (see page 158). This is a large stretch of water, and good fishing. Date of close time, from November 1st to February 2nd. Whitewell Bridge is half-a-mile below Burholme Bridge. The nearest railway station is Clitheroe, seven miles. Lees Beck enters two and a quarter miles below Whitewell Bridge, and Greystonely Beck half-a-mile still lower. Doeford Bridge is three and a half miles below Whitewell Bridge. The River Loud enters just above Doeford Bridge, and it is five miles from the bridge to Longridge, which is the nearest railway station.

From Doeford Bridge the fishing on the Lancashire side is private for the remainder of the river. On the Yorkshire side, from Doeford Bridge to the commencement of Bashall Park, tickets to fish can be had free by staying at the Red Pump Inn, near Clitheroe. Mill Brook enters a mile and a half below Doeford Bridge. Bashall Park commences three and a half miles below Doeford Bridge. From the commencement of Bashall Park to Hodder Foot the remainder of the river on the Yorkshire side can be fished by ticket, to be had free on application at the Red Lion, Clitheroe, the Three Fishes Inn, Mitton, and the Aspinall's Arms, Mitton. These tickets also allow the holder to fish a portion of the Ribble (see *post*). From the commencement of Bashall Park to Hodder Bridge is one mile, and Lower Hodder Bridge is two miles still lower. From Lower Hodder Bridge it is two and a half miles to Whalley Station. The Old Bridge is a little lower. The Hodder enters the Ribble at Hodder Foot, a mile below the bridge. The total length of the river is twenty-seven miles.

HODGE BECK.

The Hodge Beck rises at Cockayne Head, at the Head of Bransdale, and on the moors east of Bilsdale, 1,450 feet above sea level. It runs down Bransdale and Sleightholmedale to Hold Cauldron Mills, where it sinks into the ground, and rises again about two miles below at Howkeld Head. It enters the Dove about two miles south of Kirbymoorside. This stream holds some capital trout and grayling at the bottom end. Nearest railway station for the whole stream, Kirbymoorside. Best centres, Kirbymoorside and Helmsley. The whole of the fishing belongs to the Earl of Feversham with the exception of a few short breaks.

These breaks are, on the right from a little above Bransdale Castle to Low Cornfield House, a short piece near South House, and from Nawton to the Dove; and on the left a short length opposite Bransdale Castle, a short length at Brow Wood, and a length of about a mile and a quarter from Kirkdale Wood to below Welburn Bridge. Lord Feversham's water is fishable by ticket, procurable at the estate offices, Helmsley. For full particulars and restrictions see River Dove.

Bransdale Mill is three miles below the source. The fishing is of little good above this point. It is, however, included in the ticket procurable at the Helmsley estate office. Below from this point on the right side to Low Cornfield House permission to fish can be had from the tenants. Just below Bransdale Mill on the left there is a short break of fishing, about a quarter of a mile which belongs to the tenant, and then the stream is fishable by ticket from the Helmsley estate to half-a-mile below Slades Bridge. Low Cornfield House is half-a-mile below Bransdale Mill. From Low Cornfield House on the right side to Nawton, with the exception of a slight break at South House, the stream is fishable by ticket procurable at the Helmsley estate office. South House is half-a-mile below Low Cornfield House. Slades Bridge is five and a half miles below South House. Skiplam Wood commences half-a-mile below Slades Bridge, and opposite, on the left side, commences the above-mentioned break, which extends to Brow Wood, and permission to fish which is needed from the tenant. Brow Wood is a mile and a quarter below Slades Bridge. From Brow Wood to Kirkdale Wood on the left the stream is again fishable by ticket from the Helmsley estate office. Cat Hole Bridge is a mile below Brow Wood. Hold Cauldron is a mile and a quarter below Cat Hole Bridge. Here the river sinks into the ground. Skiplam Wood ends half-a-mile below. Kirkdale Wood is three-quarters of a mile below Hold Cauldron. On the left this is the end of the water fishable by ticket, and below to the confluence with the Dove permission can be had from the tenants. The bridge, which leads to Nawton on the right and Kirbymoorside on the left, is half-a-mile below Kirkdale Wood. Nawton is a mile and a half wide of the bridge, and Kirbymoorside a mile and a quarter. There are railway stations and several inns at both places. At Nawton Bridge on the right side the water fishable by ticket ends, and below to the Dove permission can be had from the tenants. Tilehouse Bridge and Howkeld Head are half-a-mile below. At Howkeld Head the stream reappears from underground. The surface bed is dry from Hold Cauldron to this point except in flood time. Welburn, where there is an inn and a bridge, is a quarter of a mile below Howkeld Head. The Hodge enters the River Dove about two miles below Welburn Bridge. The total length of the stream is seventeen and a quarter miles.

RIVER HOLME.

The River Holme runs from the Holme moors through Holmfirth Valley to the Colne at Huddersfield, a distance of eight and a half miles. Below Holme Bridge, which is about one mile from the source, the river is unfishable, on account of the pollutions. The fishable part of the stream, about one mile in extent, together with the Batley Reservoir at the head of the stream, the whole of Pinkle Beck, a tributary, and three dams at the side of the river, is in the hands of the Holme Valley Angling Club. President, Mr. Thomas E. Turner; hon. secretary, Mr. Thos Hinchcliffe, Cross-roads, Holmfirth; hon. treasurer, Mr. J. C. Barraclough. Limited to sixteen members. All trout and plenty of them. Limit eight inches. No live bait fishing allowed. Members selling their fish, or refusing to show their tickets or panniers when requested, are expelled. Entrance fee, 15s.; annual subscription, 10s. 6d. No Sunday fishing. Season commences on Good Friday, except when it happens before April 1, and ends October 1. No illegitimate fishing permitted. There is also good fishing in some of the tributaries of the Holme, but it is mostly private. Some of these tributaries feed the reservoirs already mentioned, the fishing in which belongs to the Huddersfield Angling Association. These are: the Blackmoorfoot Reservoir, which is one hundred and five acres in extent, having an altitude of 831 feet, and being four miles from Huddersfield. This Reservoir holds some good pike and perch. The nearest railway station is Netherton, on the Meltham and

Huddersfield branch. Deerhill Reservoir, forty-five acres in extent, at an altitude of 1,144 feet. Roach. Six miles from Huddersfield. Meltham nearest railway station. Holmstyes Reservoir : Trout. Eleven acres in extent. 950 feet above sea level. Eight and a half miles from Huddersfield. Holmfirth nearest station, two miles. Bawshaw Reservoir : Trout. Sixteen acres in extent. Nine and a half miles from Huddersfield. Nearest railway station, Holmfirth, three miles. Blacksike Reservoir : Trout. One acre in extent. Holmfirth, nearest station, two miles. For details see River Colne.

RIVER HULL.

The River Hull was originally a continuation of the Driffield Beck, commencing about a mile and a half above Wansford Bridge. The head of the river, as it is now known, commences at Struncheonholme Lock, seven and a half miles below its original source. This old portion of the river is dealt with in Driffield Stream and Driffield Navigation (see *ante*). Ordinary spring tides flow the whole length of the river to Struncheonholme Lock. It runs through a dead level country past Beverley and Cottingham to Hull, where it enters the Humber. The fishing above Beverley is fairly good, being confined chiefly to coarse fish, with trout in the higher reaches. The fishing is free the whole length. Below Beverley the river is polluted through the refuse from the tanneries and other places, therefore there is no fishing below Beverley except a few flounders, which come up with the tides, and are occasionally found in the lower reaches. Wilfholme Landing is two and a half miles below Strucheonholme Lock. Here there is an inn and a ferry, and it is two and a quarter miles to Lockington Station, on the Hull and Bridlington Branch. Aike Landing is two miles below Wilfholme Landing. Leven Locks are half a mile lower down. Here the Leven Canal joins the River Hull. Arram Beck is a mile and three quarters below Aike. From this point it is three-quarters of a mile to Arram Station. Hull Bridge, Tickton, is a mile and a half lower down. Beverley Beck enters a mile and three-quarters below Hull Bridge. Here the pollutions commence. They do not get up the river with the tides, however, on account of the back-water.

Beverley is half a mile wide of the river. Several inns and a railway station. Seven and a quarter miles below Beverley Brook is Cross Bridge, from which is two miles to Cottingham. Four miles lower down the river enters the Humber near the Hull Corporation Pier. The total length of the river from Struncheonhill Lock to the Humber is about twenty miles, the original length being twenty-seven and a half miles. The close time for trout is from October 15th to March 15th both inclusive. The Board of Conservators turned a quantity of yearling trout into this river at the commencement of the present season.

KINGSDALE BECK.

Kingsdale Beck has its source at Kingsdale Head, near Kingsdale House, Blackside, 1,040 feet above sea level, and is formed by the junction of Long Gill and Cluthering Gill Becks, which receive a number of small streams that drain the moors south-west of Whernside and the Blakamaya and Turbury Pastures, and the High Ridge of Gareth. There are no tributaries except the moorland ones, but these are numerous and are not fairly collected in one volume until they reach Keld Head, which, through a fault in the limestone, may be termed the real head of the stream. Keld Head is two and a half miles below Kingsdale Head, and there is no fishing above this point. The beck is an ideal trout stream and runs through a lovely valley to Ingleton, where it joins the Doe or Dale Beck in forming the River Greta. The fishing in the greater portion of these three streams is in the hands of the Ingleton Angling Association; hon. secretary, Mr. Samuel Worthington, Ingleton. Annual subscription, 5s.; boys under fifteen, 2s. 6d. Visitors' tickets are issued, fourteen days, 2s. 6d.; one day, 1s. each. The association have about nine miles of good trout water. Season commences March 1st and expires October 1st. Tickets and panniers to be shown when requested by members or watchers. Anglers are cautioned against doing damage to crops or fences. No dogs allowed. All legal baits permissible. From Keld Head to the junction with the Doe the whole of the fishing is in the hands of the Ingleton Angling Association. From

Keld Head to Long Chimney, it is a mile and a quarter. Twistleton Manor is a quarter of a mile lower down. From Keld to the junction with the Doe it is two and a quarter miles. Ingleton Bridge crosses near the junction. Their is a weir just above the bridge. There is a railway station at Ingleton. Tickets for fishing the association water can be procured from the hon. secretary, or at the Wheat Sheaf Hotel, Ingleton, where there is good accommodation for anglers.

RIVER LAVER.

The river Laver is the principal tributary of the Skell. It commences near Dallow, on the eastern edge of Dallow Gill Moors, 590 feet above the sea. Its source is formed by the confluence of the North and South Gill Becks, which run from those moors. The river winds by a very irregular and circuitous route through a charming country to the Skell, which it joins at Bishopton (see *post*). The only tributaries of note below the source are the Carlesmoor, Holborn, and Kex Becks. The fishing (all trout) is very good. The best length, which extends from Ings Bridge to the junction with the Skell, about six miles, belongs to the Ripon Club. Above Ings Bridge it is private.

Carlesmoor Beck enters on the left, two miles from the source, Laverton is a mile and a half below. Here there are inns. Gate Bridge is a mile and a half below Laverton. It is a mile and three-quarters from Gate Bridge to High Grantley, and three-quarters of a mile to Galphay. There are inns at both places. Ripon is the nearest railway station, five and three-quarter miles. Winksley is a mile and a quarter below Gate Bridge. There is an inn and it is four and a half miles to Ripon. Holborn Beck enters on the right three-quarters of a mile below Winksley, and Ings Bridge is a mile and three-quarters below that place.

From Ings Bridge to the junction with the Skell the fishing is in the hands of the Ripon Angling Club, being their best length of water. It is reserved for members of the club only, no outside tickets being issued, except to members under special circumstances as set forth in the club rules, for full details of which see the River Ure *(post)*. The club have also lengths of water on the Ure and Skell. Hon. secretary and treasurer, Arthur J. H Wood, Esq., Bellwood, Ripon. Kex Beck enters on the left, two and a half miles below Ings Bridge. Bishopton is five miles below Ings Bridge, one mile from Ripon, and two miles from Studley Royal. The Laver enters the Skell a quarter of a mile below Bishopton. The total length of the Laver is thirteen and a quarter miles.

RIVER LEVEN.

The Leven is the last of the Tees tributaries of importance. It rises on Warren Moor, on the North Cleveland Hills, 930 feet above the sea. It has a very circuitous and irregular course. The nearest railway station for the top reaches is Kildale. This is a first-class trout stream throughout, and is strictly preserved from the source to Leven Bridge, leave been difficult to obtain and very rarely granted to outsiders. Two miles and three-quarters below the source the Yorkshire and Cleveland railway crosses. Half-a-mile below is Kildale. Here there is an inn and a railway station. Easby Bridge is three and a quarter miles below Kildale. Holmes Bridge is a mile and a quarter below Easby Bridge, and Ayton Bridge is three-quarters of a mile lower. Two miles and a half below Ayton Bridge is Stokesley Bridge. There are inns and a railway station at Stokesley. Bense Bridge is a mile below Stokesley Bridge. Six miles below Bense Bridge is Sexhow Hall. From this point it is one mile to Sexhow Station. Hutton Bridge is half-a-mile lower down. Rudby stands on the opposite bank to Hutton. From the bridge it is a mile and a quarter to Potto Station. Crathorne Bridge is three miles below Hutton Bridge. There is an inn at Crathorne, and it is one and a half miles to Picton Junction Station. Two miles and a quarter below Crathorne Bridge is Foxton Bridge, and four miles below Foxton Bridge is Leven Bridge. At Leven Bridge there is a dam, and the river is tidal below this point. From Leven Bridge to the Tees the fishing on the right bank is private. From the bridge downwards on the left bank Mr. Wm. Farnby, of the Cross Keys, has about half-a-mile of fishing. This is the landlord's private water, and holds some good trout. He grants permission to parties calling at his house.

Below the Cross Keys water to the Tees the fishing is private. The Cross Keys is near Leven Bridge. From the bridge it is two miles to Yarm Station. Besides trout, roach, chub, and eels, flounders are plentiful in the tide-way. A mile and a half below Leven Bridge the river enters the Tees about one mile below Yarm. The total length of the river is twenty-nine and a quarter miles.

RIVER LUNE.

The River Lune commences at Wath, in the county of Westmoreland, and is a continuation of the Greenside and Scanwith Becks, which run from Ravenstonedale. The river flows due west to Tebay, receiving in its course numerous tributaries from Langdale Fell and the Orton and Raisbeck Moors. From Tebay it runs due south, not receiving many tributaries until it approaches Lowgill, when they become both numerous and important to below the confluence with the River Wenning. The Borrow Beck joins eight miles from the source, and this is the most important tributary above Sedbergh. The Lune first joins the county of York at Gibbet Hill, on the north-west slope of Lingshaw Fell, and nine and three-quarter miles from the source. Thence it forms the county boundary for seven and a quarter miles, running along the western foot of Lowgill Fells. Seventeen miles from the source of the Lune the River Rawthey enters (see *post*). This is a most important angling tributary, and receives two other first-class Yorkshire angling streams in the rivers Clough and Dee (see *post*). At Rawthey Mouth the Lune leaves the county of York and runs south by Kirkby Lonsdale, Tunstall, and Hornby. Below Tunstall, and thirty-two miles from source of Lune the River Greta enters (see *ante*), and below Hornby, two and three-quarter miles lower down, the River Wenning enters (see *post*). From Wenning Mouth the Lune flows by Halton and Lancaster to the sea, six miles south of Morecambe. The total length of the river is fifty-four miles. The Lunesdale Fish Hatchery, an extensive fish breeding establishment, is situate at Halton ; hon. secretary, Mr. W. Appleyard, Lancaster (see page 158).

The trout fishing on the Lune is good, and the salmon fishing fairly decent. The highest salmon net on the river is a little above Rawthey Mouth, and as the salmon can get up the whole length of the river, even as far as Ravenstonedale, the rod fishing is good. Unfortunately the salmon season is a short one, as they do not come up this part of the river until September, and the river suffers materially from snatching and spearing in the close time. The close season for salmon is November 15 to March 1; and trout, October 2 to March 1. Salmon rod licence, 20s.; trout, 2s. 6d. Other restrictions in accordance with the Fisheries Board. So far as the Yorkshire portion of the Lune is concerned, it is practically open fishing on both sides from Gibbet Hill to the Lowgill Viaduct (two and a quarter miles). Below to the railway viaduct, two miles lower down, leave to fish is readily granted by the tenants. From the viaduct to Rawthey Mouth, the river is private on both sides. Anglers are not interfered with on the top portion so long as they conduct themselves properly, though it must be understood that the owners and tenants have power to stop them. Good salmon are caught in September and October, and the trout average about three to the pound. The river runs down a beautiful valley, which is inclosed by high mountains, the stream falling over a rocky limestone bed in a succession of streams and pools. The nearest railway stations are Lowgill and Sedbergh, the latter being the best centre. Lowgill Station is one mile and a quarter below Gibbet Hill. Lowgill Beck enters one mile and three-quarters below the station. This stream holds some nice fish and is also open. The railway viaduct is a mile and three-quarters below. Lincoln's Inn Bridge is about a quarter of a mile below the viaduct. From the bridge it is one and three-quarter miles to Sedbergh. Here there are inns and a railway station. About a mile below Lincoln's Inn Bridge is Killington New Bridge. Here the Sedbergh and Lancaster highway crosses the river. It is two and a half miles to Sedbergh. A mile lower down, the River Rawthey enters the Lune near Marthwaite New Bridge. The river watcher is William Holmes, High Oaks, Sedbergh.

RIVER LUNE (TEESDALE).

The River Lune starts at Grains o' th' Beck Bridge, 1,173 feet above sea level, and is formed by Long Grain and Lune Head Becks. The former receives the Arngill Beck, which runs from

Arngill Fish Pond, and Force, Philip Reed, and Keekham Becks. The latter receives the Cleve Beck and other small streams. The whole drain the Lune Forest and Romaldkirk Moors. The Middleton and Brough highway runs parallel with the river. The nearest railway station is Middleton-in-Teesdale. Lunedale is very picturesque, and this magnificent trout stream is one of the most important tributaries of the Tees. It is the property of Lord Strathmore, but the sporting rights are at present rented by Lord Westbury, therefore the fishing is private. A mile and a half below the source there is a waterfall, and a mile and a half still lower Thwaites Bridge crosses. A mile and a half below Thwaites Bridge is Grassholme Bridge, and just above this latter bridge is a weir. Two and a half miles below Grassholme Bridge the Teesdale Valley Railway Bridge crosses, and just below this is Lune Bridge, from which it is one mile to Middleton Station. Half-a-mile below Lune Bridge is a weir, and half-a-mile lower the Lune joins the Tees. The total length of the stream is eight and a quarter miles.

MAIZE BECK.

Maize Beck, an important angling tributary of the Tees, has its source in Westmoreland, at Great Rundale Tarn, which lies north of Backstone Edge. It receives numerous mountain tributaries, and drains the country lying between Dufton Fells, Morton Fells, and Mickle Fell. The fishing in the higher reaches is not much good, but after the stream joins the county of York then the trout fishing is very good. Permission to fish the stream can be had from Mr. J. C. Barker, Langdon Beck Hotel, who grants tickets to visitors to his house (see the River Tees). Four miles from the source Swarth Becks and Fishers' Sike join the stream, and half-a-mile lower down it joins the county of York. From this point to the Tees it forms the county boundary. A mile and a half lower down is Maize Beck Bridge, and four miles and a half below the bridge the stream enters the Tees just below Caldron Snout. A road runs parallel with the stream the whole way. Middleton-in-Teesdale, eight and a half miles, is the nearest railway station. The total length of Maize Beck is ten and a half miles.

MALTBY DYKE.

Maltby Dyke has its source about three-quarters of a mile west of Maltby, near to the Rotherham and Maltby highway. It is formed by the junction of Newhall Dyke, Hellaby Brook, and Kingsforth Brook, which drain the Stanton-cum-Hellaby district. Maltby is six miles from Rotherham. The stream enters the Roche Abbey grounds about two and a quarter miles from its source. It is only a small stream, but below the abbey it widens out into an elongated pond, about a quarter of a mile long, at the foot of which is another pond of a similar length. Between the two ponds a stream enters, which runs from another large pond. These ponds are all within the abbey grounds. Three miles and a half from its source the stream below is called Firbeck Dyke, and Sandbeck Park lies on the left bank. A mile and a quarter lower down it enters Firbeck Park, and soon runs to the Old Mill Dam, within the park. This dam receives the stream from the fish ponds in Firbeck Park, The stream crosses the county boundary five miles and three-quarters from its source, and runs to the River Ryton. The stream and the whole of the ponds hold fish, trout and roach, and the fishing throughout is first-class. The fishing, however, is private, but permission in some instances is occasionally granted.

RIVER NIDD.

The River Nidd has its source at Nidd Head Spring, on Great Whernside, 2,000 feet above the sea. Here numerous small moorland streams drain Nidd Head allotment into the main stream, whilst a little lower down, but above Angram, other streams drain the Angram Pastures on Little Whernside on the Black Fell Pastures, the principal of the latter being Stone Beck, which flows from Stone Head Pasture on Great Whernside, and joins the Nidd at Angram. The other tributaries of the Nidd are very numerous in the whole of its course as far down as Walshford Bridge, where they cease. The principal of these tributaries are the How Stean,

Oak Beck (see *post*), and the River Crimple (see *ante*). How Stean Beck, which is a first-class angling stream, but strictly private, is formed by Blooming Gill, Strait Stean, and Bakestone Gill Becks, which rise on Rigg's Moor. How Stean joins the Nidd below Lofthouse.

The Nidd runs through a variety of country commencing with high moorlands, and moving thence through Nidderdale, "the Switzerland of England." one of the most picturesque valleys of the north, until below Ribston it enters upon the skirts of the vale of York, a flat, monotonous country. At Manchester Hole, and Goyden Pot, above Lofthouse, the river enters the ground, and does not reappear for two and three quarter miles, when it rises again, after traversing a subterranean passage, at Nidd's Head, a short distance wide of the river. Goyden Pot is an immense cavern, forty feet below the surface. The river rushes along the bottom, and the magnitude of the cavern is very grand and awe-inspiring. When there is a heavy rainfall, however, the cavern is filled, and the crowded floods roll down the regular course, which at other times is dry. The river is a succession of streams and pools until Killinghall Bridge is reached, then come several deeps until below Ribston, when it becomes a narrow, sluggish, winding stream, dragging its slow course through the deep, sedgy banks to the Ouse. The fishing is good throughout its entire length. The top reaches are confined entirely to trout. Grayling are found between Pateley Bridge and Killinghall Bridge, also chub, dace, and eels. Below Killinghall to Ribston it is mixed fishing, there being a fair supply of trout, and below Walshford Bridge all kinds of coarse fish are found, and an occasional trout. There is practically no open fishing on the Nidd where game fish are to be found, the best of the fishing being strictly preserved by the owners.

Angram is two miles and a half below Nidd Head Spring. West House stands opposite. Low Wood-dale Bridge is three miles below Angram, and New Houses Bridge is a mile further down. Half-a-mile below New Houses Bridge is Manchester Holes, where the river enters the ground. Above this point there is nothing but small fish. Goyden Pot Hole is a quarter of a mile below Manchester Holes, and Lofthouse is two miles below. There is an inn at Lofthouse, also at Middlesmoor, which is half-a-mile from Lofthouse Bridge. The mail cart carries passengers from these places to Pateley Bridge, about seven miles. The highway runs parallel with the river. How Stean Beck, a private angling stream, enters half-a-mile below Lofthouse Bridge. Above this point at ordinary times the bed of the river is dry to Manchester Holes. The fishing no good above Lofthouse. From Lofthouse to Killinghall Bridge, a distance of twenty miles, the fishing is in the hands of the owners, from whom permission must be obtained. The principal of these are Mr. T. E. Yorke, of Bewerley Hall; and Mr. George Metcalfe, of Castlestead, Pateley Bridge; Sir Henry Ingilby, Bart., of Ripley Castle; Colonel Chas. S. Greenwood, of Swarcliffe Hall; and the Rev. Thos. Sheepshanks, M.A., of Arthington Hall. These gentlemen or their stewards do occasionally grant permission to fish some portions of their water. A little below How Stean Beck the river re-enters its course by a stream which runs from Nidd Heads, which rise in a field about 200 yards wide of the main river. Ramsgill Bridge is two and a half miles below Lofthouse. There is an inn at Ramsgill. Wath Bridge three and a half miles below Ramsgill. Pateley Bridge is one and three-quarter miles below Wath. There is a weir just above Pateley Bridge. There are several inns at Pateley. Good accommodation for anglers will be found at the Crown, where Mrs. King is an exceptional landlady. Pateley Bridge is the best centre for the best fishing on the Nidd.

Pateley railway station is the highest in Nidderdale. The Nidd valley railway runs through the vale to Harrogate. The Harrogate, Knaresborough, and York branch runs almost parallel with the remainder of the river. Bewerley Hall and Castlestead stand wide of the river, about half-a-mile below the bridge. Most of the fishing above Pateley Bridge belongs to Mr. T. E. Yorke. Mr. Metcalfe's fishing is near to Castlestead. A mile below Pateley Bridge there is a weir, and just below this the top portion of Sir Henry Ingilby's fishing commences, and extends to Darley Beck. Glass House Bridge is a mile and a quarter below Pateley Bridge. Smelt House is a mile and a quarter below Glass House Bridge. A quarter of a mile below Smelt House there is a weir, another a quarter of a mile below that, and a third a quarter of a mile lower still, at New York Flax Mills. Summer Bridge is half-a-mile below the Flax Mill. There is a weir just above the bridge, and it is a quarter of a mile from the bridge to Dacre Banks Station. There is an inn at Dacre Banks. Darley Beck enters on the right a mile and three-quarters below Summer Bridge. The Harrogate Conservative Angling Association have the privilege of fishing the length of water at Dacre Banks, which lies between Summer Bridge and Darley, and belongs to Mr. Samson Fox, see Oak Beck *(post)*. This is the end of the first length of Sir Henry Ingilby's water. At Clough Gill, on the left, which is a mile below Summer Bridge, Mr. Swires' fishing commences, and runs to the commencement of Swarcliffe Plantation, which is three and a half miles below Summer Bridge. At Swarcliffe Plantation Colonel Greenwood's water commences and runs to the island below Hampsthwaite Bridge. New Bridge is three-quarters of a mile below Swarcliffe Plantation, and Wreaks Bridge is another three-quarters below New Bridge. At Wreaks Bridge is Birstwith Station, also an inn. It is a quarter of a mile to Birstwith, and half-a-mile to Swarcliffe Hall. There is a weir just above the bridge and also below the bridge. Hampsthwaite Bridge is a mile and a quarter below Wreaks Bridge. At Hampsthwaite there are inns and a railway station. It is half-a-mile from the bridge to the island where Colonel Greenwood's water ends. At this point, on the right, Mr. Sheepshanks' water commences, and extends for about a mile. The Harrogate Conservative Angling Association have the privilege of fishing the water on both sides from Hampsthwaite Bridge to Killinghall Bridge (For particulars see Oak Beck). On the left Sir Henry Ingilby comes in again and extends to Killinghall Bridge, as he also does on the right from the bottom of Mr. Sheepshanks' water. Killinghall Bridge is about three miles below Hampsthwaite Bridge. It is half-a-mile to Ripley, where there is an inn. The railway station is near the bridge. It is also half-a-mile from the bridge to Killinghall, where there are inns, and the highway leads to Harrogate, two and a quarter miles. There is a weir at Killinghall Bridge and another weir half-a-mile lower down. The limit for trout on Sir Henry Ingilby's water is 7in.

The Knaresborough Anglers' Club water commences at Killinghall Bridge, and extends on both sides to Ribston, a distance of thirteen miles. President, the Hon. and Rev. Canon Lascelles; Mr. Alfred Walton, treasurer; Mr. Fred Wolstenholme, hon. secretary; and Mr. J. G. Brown, High Street, Knaresborough, acting secretary. River watcher, William Todd, High Street, Knaresborough. The club is limited to thirty-five members. Annual subscription: honorary members, £1; fishing members, £1 10s. No short period tickets are issued. Dates of close time from September 16th to March 15th inclusive. Limit for trout, 8 inches. No minnow fishing allowed until after May 1st, after that date all legal baits permitted.

Oak Beck (see *post*) enters a mile and three-quarters below Killinghall Bridge. Near Oak Beck the railway from Harrogate to Ripon crosses. Three-quarters of a mile below there is a weir and a ford to Bilton. The Harrogate Conservation Angling Association have the privilege of fishing Mr. B. T. Wood's water at Knaresborough (for details see Oak Beck). Knaresborough High Bridge is five and three-quarter miles below Killinghall Bridge. From here the highway to Harrogate is three miles. There are several inns and a railway station at Knaresborough. The York and Harrogate branch railway bridge crosses just below the High Bridge. There is a weir a quarter of a mile below the bridge. The Low Bridge is nearly three-quarters of a mile below the High Bridge. From the Low Bridge the highway leads to Spofforth and Wetherby, and a quarter of a mile below there is a weir. Abbey Mill Weir and Plompton Mill Weir are a mile and a quarter below Low Bridge, and Grimbald Bridge is a mile and a half. A mile and three-quarters below Grimbald Bridge is Goldsborough Mill Weir and ford. From this point it is two miles to Goldsborough Station. There are inns at Goldsborough. Ribston Park commences two miles and a quarter below Goldsborough Mill. Here the Knaresborough Anglers' Club water ends on the left, and a mile lower down on the right at Little Ribston.

From the bottom limit of the Knaresborough Club length to the end of Aubert Pasture at Cattal, permission to fish on both sides of the river must be had from the owners or tenants. On the Ribston Park side, Mr. J. Dent Dent gives leave to anglers with whom he is acquainted, but on the opposite side permission is more easily obtained. There is a bridge at Ribston Park which crosses the river to Little Ribston. This leads to the highway to Wetherby, which is the nearest station, three and a half miles. The River Crimple (see *ante*) enters the Nidd a mile and a half below Ribston. Walshford Bridge is two miles and a quarter below Ribston. At Walshford there is an inn. Here the Great North Road crosses the river. It is three and a quarter miles to Wetherby Station, and two miles to Allerton Station on the York and Harrogate branch. Cowthorpe is a mile and a quarter below Walshford Bridge. There is a weir at Cowthorpe. Hunsingore is a mile and a half below Walshford Bridge, and Cattal Bridge is a mile and a quarter below Hunsingore. From Cattal it is a mile and a quarter to the railway station. Aubert or Horbalt Pasture is half-a-mile below the bridge. From this point to the confluence with the Ouse, permission to fish is easily obtained from the tenants, in fact in most places anglers are not interfered with so long as they conduct themselves properly and do no damage. It is mainly coarse fishing and fairly good. Kirk Hammerton is three miles below Cattal, and half-a-mile wide of the river. There is an inn, also a railway station. A quarter of a mile below there is Mill Bridge, and a weir above the bridge. Three miles and a quarter below Mill Bridge Skip Bridge railway bridge crosses the river, and half-a-mile lower down is Skip Bridge. Here the York and Boroughbridge highway crosses. It is half-a-mile from the bridge to the inn, and two and a quarter miles to Marston Station on the one hand, and one mile to Kirk Hammerton Station on the other. Moor Monkton is three and a quarter miles below Skip Bridge. There is an inn, and it is one and a half miles to Marston Station. A mile and a half below Moor Monkton the Nidd joins the Ouse. At Nidd Mouth there are ferries both across the Nidd and the Ouse. Nun Monkton stands at the junction of the rivers. There are inns. From the ferry a bridle road skirts Beningbrough Park down the Ouse to Warp Gate, thence to Beningbrough Lodge and Shipton railway station, two and a quarter miles. The total length of the River Nidd is fifty-nine and a quarter miles.

"**THE NIDD**" (No. 2 of the Yorkshire Rivers Series), with bird's-eye view of the roads and surrounding country, by Tom Bradley, being a most complete angler's or tourist's guide, showing all places of note on the banks of the river, with brief descriptions of the legends and folk lore of the district. May be obtained at the office of *The Yorkshire Post*, Leeds, or ordered through any bookseller, price 6d., by post 7½d.

OAK BECK.

Oak Beck, an important angling tributary of the Nidd, is a continuation of Scargill Beck which rises at Broad Dub, Haverah Park, 700 feet above sea level. After running north to Scargill plantation it turns due east past Low Boar Hole to Pot Bridge, thence in a north-easterly direction past Birch Craggs, Oakden, Little Wonder, and Knox Mills to the Nidd below Bilton. Harrogate is the best centre and the nearest railway station. Broad Dub, the source of the stream, is five and three-quarter miles from Harrogate. From the source to Pot Bridge, four and a quarter miles following the windings of the stream, the fishing is private. Beaver Dyke enters a mile and a half below the source and holds some nice fish. At Pot Bridge the Killinghall T.P. Road crosses. It is three and a quarter miles to Harrogate. From Pot Bridge to the beginning of Harrogate Corporation Farm, about one mile, the fishing is in the hands of the Harrogate Conservative Angling Association. Patron, J. L. Wharton, Esq., M.P.; president, Samson Fox, Esq., C.E., J.P.; hon. secretary, Mr. T. Cartman, Montpelier Parade, Harrogate; hon. treasurer, Mr. G. Lamb. Annual subscription, honorary members, 10s.; ordinary members, 5s.; with 5s. entrance fee. Limited to sixty-five ordinary members. Restrictions in accordance with the Yorkshire Fishery Board Regulations. Limit for trout and grayling, 7in. Visitors admitted on payment of annual subscription and entrance fee. Members have the privilege of inviting a friend to fish in the club waters provided he be accompanied by a member of the club and does not reside within five miles of Harrogate and be approved by any two members of the committee. This club, which is but recently formed, have a fish hatchery and rearing ponds at Oakdale, and they intend to keep their water well stocked. They have also permission to fish a stretch of water in the Nidd at Dacre Banks, also Mr. Sheepshanks' water lower down the Nidd, and Mr. B. T. Wood's water at Knaresborough on the same river; likewise Mr. Hawkins' water on the Ure at Boroughbridge, below the bridge, and a length of the Crimple between Guilders' Bridge and Spofforth. From the bottom limit of this club's water to Harrogate it is one mile.

From the top boundary of the Harrogate Corporation Farm to the Gas Works, about a mile and three-quarters, the fishing belongs to the Harrogate Angling Association, for particulars see River Crimple. This club have recently re-stocked their length on Oak Beck with yearling trout. They have also good lengths of water on the Crimple, and on the Ure at Boroughbridge, from the bridge on the north side to two hundred yards below Milby Lock. From the Gas Works it is one mile to Low Harrogate. Below the Gas Works to the Nidd the fishing in Oak Beck belongs to the farmers, and is little good on account of the poaching and pollutions. Knox Bridge is half-a-mile below the Gas Works. From this bridge it is a mile to Killinghall, and a mile and a half to Harrogate. The beck enters the Nidd one mile below this bridge, and one and three-quarter miles below Killinghall Bridge. The total length of the stream is eight and a half miles.

RIVER OUSE.

The Ouse is formed by the confluence of the Swale and the Ure. It also receives in its course to the Humber, the Nidd, the Foss, the Wharfe, the Derwent, the Aire and Calder, and the Don. Thus it will be seen that most of the Yorkshire Rivers flow to the Ouse. Being a tidal river, its general aspect below Goole savours more of the sea than an inland water. It is a flat, slow-flowing river, navigable the whole length, and without a stream in its entire course. The banks are deep, and in many places treacherous. There is a towing-path by one or the other bank all the way from Swale Nab to Goole. The tide flows to Naburn Lock. Before this dam was constructed it flowed the whole length of the river.

The fishing, except the salmon (which is let to professional fishermen), is almost entirely free from end to end. There are no trout in the Ouse, or at least they are very rare; but salmon abound at certain seasons. Coarse fish are plentiful. Chub, roach, dace, pike, eels, bream, and flounders and other salt-water fish in the lower reaches. The half of the river above Naburn Lock affords the best sport. Below Naburn Lock, in the Lock and Moreby reaches, there is good fishing for chub and roach. The Acaster and Naburn reaches are noted for chub and dace, and there are some good bream holes in the Bishopthorpe and Fulford reaches. About the City of York there is some good roach fishing, and barbel are found close to the Scarborough Bridge. The best chub fishing is at Poppleton, and pike in Benningbrough and Monkton deeps. The holes below Linton Lock are noted for barbel. Above Linton Lock there are both pike and barbel, but the fishing is not very good. It improves above Aldwark and Lower Dunsforth.

The Ouse commences at Swale Nab. The coarse fishing is free on sufferance on the right as far as Aldwark Bridge (four miles), and on the left as far as York (eighteen miles). Anglers are expected to keep out of the land when crops are on. Lower Dunsforth is three-quarters of a mile below Swale Nab, and three and a half miles from Boroughbridge Station. Aldwark is three and a half miles below Swale Nab, and three and three-quarter miles from Alne railway station. There are inns at both places. The fishing on the right from Aldwark to Linton Ferry (three miles) is in the hands of the tenants, from whom permission may be obtained. Linton-upon-Ouse stands on the opposite bank. Here there is an inn, and the nearest railway station is Tollerton Lanes, three and a quarter miles. The fishing on the right from Linton Ferry to the mouth of the Nidd (two and three-quarter miles) is private. Linton Lock is a quarter of a mile below Linton Ferry, and the River Kyle enters a mile below the ferry. Newton-upon-Ouse, where there are inns, is one and a quarter miles below Linton Ferry. The nearest railway station is Shipton, three miles. Benningbrough Park commences just below Newton, but there is a towing-path between the park and the river, from which one may fish without trespassing in the park.

Nun Monkton stands on the right bank at the mouth of the Nidd. Here there are inns, also a ferry. The railway stations are Kirk Hammerton (three and a half miles) and Marston (two and a half miles). There is good pike and chub fishing about the mouth of the Nidd. From Nidd Mouth to Poppleton Ferry, on the right (three and three-quarter miles), the fishing is free on sufferance. In Monkton Reach, below Nun Monkton, there is good roach and dace fishing and a few perch. Beningbrough is two miles and a quarter below Nun Monkton Ferry. The nearest railway station is Shipton, one and a half miles. Opposite Poppleton Ferry is Skelton, where there is an inn. There are also inns at Poppleton, which is a favourite resort of anglers. The fishing from Poppleton, on the right side of the river to Scarborough Railway Bridge, York, is private. The fishing in the vicinity of York City is all open. Good roach and barbel fishing near to the Scarborough Railway Bridge. From York to Bishopthorpe Palace Grounds, on the right (three miles), the fishing is open, likewise on the left to Water Fulford (two and a quarter miles). At Fulford there are inns, and here the Fulford Hall Estates commences. Permission to fish can be obtained from Captain Key by all *bona fide* anglers. There are some good bream holes on the Fulford Estate.

At Bishopthorpe, which is two miles from Copmanthorpe Station, there are inns. The fishing adjoining the palace grounds is private. There is a ferry at Bishopthorpe, from which point on the left to the lower boundary of Moreby Park (three and a half miles) the fishing is private. On the right, from Bishopthorpe Ferry, the coarse fishing is open the whole way to the mouth of the river, except where private grounds intervene. Naburn village is one and a half miles below Bishopthorpe. Here there are inns and a railway station. Acaster Malbis, which is a popular angling resort, is half-a-mile below Naburn, on the opposite bank. Here there is an inn. Copmanthorpe (one and three-quarter miles) being the nearest railway station. There is good roach and dace fishing at Acaster. Naburn Lock is a mile below Naburn. Below the weir at this point the river is tidal. From the end of Moreby Park on the left, to the river's mouth, the coarse fishing is free except where private grounds intervene. The salmon fishing is strictly private. Acaster Ferry is a mile and three-quarters below Moreby Park. Acaster Selby stands on the right bank. Bolton Percy railway station is three and a half miles distant. On the left it is one mile to Stillingfleet, where there is an inn, and two and a half miles to Escrick Station.

Below Low Acaster Reach the coarse fishing is open on both sides to the Humber, except where private grounds intervene. The salmon fishing is strictly private. Stillingfleet Beck enters about three-quarters of a mile below Acaster. Stillingfleet, one of the loveliest villages in Yorkshire, is a mile wide of the river. The River Wharfe enters a mile and a quarter below Stillingfleet Beck (see *post*). Cawood Bridge is three-quarters of a mile below Wharfe Mouth. At Cawood there are several inns, the nearest railway station on the right bank being Selby, four and a quarter miles, and on the left, Riccall, three and a quarter miles. Kelfield is a mile and a quarter below Cawood, and Riccall Landing a mile and a quarter below Kelfield. Riccall is half-a-mile wide of the river. Here there are inns and a railway station. Wistow Landing is a mile below Riccall Landing. Wistow is one mile from the river, and two and a half miles from Selby, which is the nearest railway station. There are inns at both places. The coarse fishing is chiefly eels and flounders. Barlby is two and three-quarter miles below Wistow Landing.

Selby is a mile and a half below Barlby. Here there are several inns and a railway station. Selby is one of the principal shipping stations on the river. It stands on the Leeds, Selby, and Hull Railway. The coarse fishing is fairly good, eels principally. Just below Selby, the Selby Canal, which runs from the Aire at West Haddesley, joins the Ouse. Cliffe Landing is five miles below Selby. Cliffe is three-quarters of a mile wide of the river. Inns and railway stations. Hemingbrough is three-quarters of a mile below Cliffe Landing. Several inns at Hemingbrough, and a mile and a quarter below which place the River Derwent (see *ante*) enters on the left bank. Just below Derwent Mouth is Drax Ferry. Long Drax, where there is a railway station, is one mile and three-quarters wide of the river. On the opposite bank it is two and a quarter miles to Wressil Station, and a quarter of a mile to Barmby, where there are inns. Three and a half miles below Derwent Mouth is Asselby Island. Asselby is three-quarters of a mile wide of the river. The River Aire (polluted) enters on the right side opposite the low end of Asselby Island. The fishing for a considerable distance below this point is no good on account of the pollutions from the Aire. The destruction of salmon by these pollutions during the past season has been very great. Booth Ferry is three-quarters of a mile below Asselby Island, from which place it is half-a-mile to Airmyn, two miles to Goole, and one and a half miles to Howden. There is an inn at Booth Ferry, two miles and a quarter below which place is Howden Dyke Ferry, from which it is one mile to Howden, where there are several inns and two railway stations. Kilpin Pike stands near the ferry. Hook is three-quarters of a mile below Howden Dyke Ferry. Skelton stands on the opposite bank, from which place it is one and a half miles to Laxton Station.

Goole is nearly two miles below Hook. This is a seaport where there are extensive docks, numerous inns, and a railway station. Below Goole the river is very wide and partakes more of the sea than an inland stream. There is some fairly good fishing for eels and flounders, &c., from the piers, jetties, and breakwaters on both sides to the mouth of the river. Free the whole length, except salmon fishing, which is strictly private.

The Dutch River (River Don, see *ante*) enters on the right side at Old Goole. A steam-packet carries passengers from Goole to the places down the river. Swinefleet, on the right bank, is a mile and a quarter below Goole; Saltmarshe, on the left bank, four miles. It is one mile from the latter place to Laxton railway station. There are inns at both places. Reedness on the right, and Cotness on the left, are four and a half miles below Goole. Whitgift, on the right, where there is an inn, is five and a half miles, and Yokefleet, on the left, is six and a half miles. Ousefleet, on the right, is seven and a quarter miles, and Blacktoft, on the left, is eight miles. At the latter place there is an inn, and it is three miles to Staddlethorpe, the nearest railway station. There is decent fishing at those places. At nine and a quarter miles below Goole at Trent Falls and Faxfleet, the Ouse joins the Trent, and forms the River Humber. The total length of the Ouse from source to mouth is sixty-three and a half miles.

"**THE OUSE**" (No 5 of the Yorkshire Rivers Series), with bird's-eye view of the roads and surrounding country, by Tom Bradley, being a most complete angler's or tourist's guide, showing all places of note on the banks of the river, with brief descriptions of the legends and folk lore of the district. May be obtained at the office of *The Yorkshire Post*, Leeds, or ordered through any bookseller, price 6d., by post 7½d.

PICKERING BECK.

Pickering Beck may be said to have its source in Eller Beck, near Eller Bridge, on the Pickering and Whitby Turnpike Road, which crosses the Goathland Moors at this point. At the place where it joins or leaves Eller Beck it is 520 feet above the sea level. Eller Beck runs from Lilla Howe due west to the Goathland valley; thence down the valley due north to Beck Hole, where it is joined by West Beck, the two forming the Murk Esk, which runs to the River Esk at Grosmont. The top end of Pickering Beck is almost a dead level, that is at Fen Bogs, and in the flood times the water runs both ways. Thus it will be seen that although the beck actually runs to the Costa, and thence by the Rye to the Derwent, it is also connected, as shown above, with the Esk, which runs to the sea at Whitby. Pickering Beck runs through a most charming valley from its source to Pickering. It is wild and rugged at the top end, but very picturesque, nevertheless. A little above Levisham it enters Newton Dale, and runs thence to Pickering through a green glade bordered on either hand by rising woodlands. From Pickering to Costa Beck the country through which the stream runs is a dead level, and from Ings Bridge to the Costa it is a deep, slow-running water, between high flood banks. Eller Beck Bridge is ten miles from Whitby and eleven from Pickering. The highway runs parallel with the stream, and the railway—the Whitby and Pickering branch—lies contiguous to it from Pickering to the source.

The members of the Pickering Club claim that there is no better trout or grayling stream in Yorkshire, particularly the bottom end, which is the club length, and that it is quite fishable on any day, no single day being wrong. The fish are splendid in quality and large in size. The best length for trout is from Vivers Mill to Low Mill, and for grayling from Low Mill to the Costa. There are very few other fish. The fishing above Farwath is free, but except for four or five miles above that place they run very small, and it is not up to much. From Farwarth to the weir, above Pickering, it is under the control of the Duchy, and then below through the town of Pickering to Vivers Mill it is free again. At Vivers Mill the Pickering Fishery Association water commences, and runs to the Costa.

Newton Dale commences five and three-quarter miles below the source. Newton is a mile lower down. On the opposite side of the beck is Levisham Station ; Levisham is three-quarters of a mile wide of the stream. Farwath Bridge is two miles below Newton. Here the first portion of the open fishing ends, and below to the weir above Pickering, it is under the control of the Duchy. Blansby Park Wood commences at Farwath Bridge, and extends for three miles down stream. Levisham Beck enters at Farwath. Little Park Wood commences a mile and three-quarters below Farwath, and extends for two miles down stream. The weir above Pickering is four and a quarter miles below Farwath. From the weir to Vivers Mill (one mile) the fishing is free. Pickering is half-a-mile below the weir. This is the best centre. There are several inns and a railway station.

From Vivers Mill to the junction with the Costa the fishing is in the hands of the Pickering Fishery Association, president, Robert Fletcher, Esq. There is a committee composed of the land-owners, also an acting committee. Treasurer, Mr. James Smith ; secretary, Mr. Jno. S. Guffick ; assistant secretary, Mr. J. W. Weldon ; beck watcher, Wm. Smith, of Harome, now residing at Pickering. Each land-owner is entitled to a certain number of tickets in proportion to the amount of frontage he owns. Parishioners of Pickering may fish between Vivers Mill and Low Mill by paying 2s. 6d. a year, or the whole length of the association water on payment of 10s. per annum. Outsiders: season tickets, 20s.; fortnightly, 7s. 6d.; daily, 2s. Obtainable from the secretary, Mr. John S. Guffick, Burgate, Pickering, or Mr. H. Coverdale, Market Place, and Mr. W. Fletcher, Post Office, Pickering. Membership not limited; only one rod allowed. All legitimate baits permitted from Vivers Mill to the Low Mill. Artificial fly only below the Low Mill until after July 1st, when minnow fishing is allowed until October 1st. No ground baiting allowed. Worm fishing for grayling permitted from October 1st to February 1st. No Sunday fishing. No trout or grayling to be taken under nine inches. Trout fishing commences from April 1st, closes October 1st. Grayling season commences June 16th, closes February 1st. Tickets and panniers to be shown on demand to landowners, members, and keepers. The tickets will be forfeited by any infringement of the rules. No member or subscriber to fish more than thirty days between April 1st and October 1st inclusive.

Low Mill is three-quarters of a mile below Vivers Mill, and the stream enters the Costa two and a half miles below Low Mill, and near to Kirby Misperton Bridge, Kirby Misperton Bridge is a quarter of a mile distant. There is an inn. The nearest railway stations are Marishes-road and Pickering. The total length of the stream is seventeen and a quarter miles.

RIVER RAWTHEY.

The River Rawthey rises 2,155 feet above sea level on East Baugh Fell, near Knoutberry Haw, and makes a circular course right round the West Baugh Fells and Blue Castor to Sedbergh, where it enters the Lune. The principal tributaries are the Dee and the Clough River (see *ante*), which enter the lower part of the Rawthey, and are both good angling streams. There are, however, numerous tributaries which in the top reaches drain the above hills, and the Holmes Moss and Uldale Moors, and in the middle and lower reaches the Cautley and Sedbergh Moors and the south side of Ravenstonedale Common. The principal of these are the Middlehouse Gill Beck, Sally Beck, Wandale Beck, Backside Beck, Hobdale Beck and Hebblethwaite Beck, all holding fish, the fishing being open. The river from its source to Uldale Bridge is in the county of York; but from Uldale Bridge to High Haygarth it forms the boundary between the counties of York and Westmoreland. From High Haygarth to Brig it is in Yorkshire again, and from Brig Flats to the Lune it once more forms the boundary between Yorkshire and Westmoreland. The river above High Haygarth runs through a wild mountainous country, and below that point it enters a deep valley enclosed by high mountains, but very beautiful nevertheless. The fishing is good throughout. There is nothing but salmon and trout. The salmon do not get higher up than the weir at Birks Mill. The whole of the fishing above this weir to the river's source is practically open. Anglers are not molested so long as they conduct themselves like *bona fide* sportsmen. Below Birks Mill to where the river enters the Lune, the fishing on both sides is private, except about a quarter of a mile on the left bank, which is open from Dee Mouth to the railway viaduct where the Ingleton and Tebay branch crosses the river. The close season for salmon is November 15th to March 1st; for trout, October 2nd to March 1st. Salmon rod licence 20s., trout, 2s. 6d., other restrictions in accordance with the Fisheries Board Regulations. Trout are found in the highest reaches of the river. River watcher, William Holmes, High Oaks, Sedbergh. Sedbergh is the nearest railway station and the best centre. Uldale Bridge is four miles from the source. Here the Middlehouse Gill Beck enters. Hall Intake Bridge is half-a-mile lower down, and Words Intake Bridge half-a-mile still lower. Immediately below this bridge is Rawthey Bridge. Here the Sedbergh to Kirkby Stephen highway crosses the river. This highway runs parallel with the stream to Sedbergh. Sally Beck enters here. Three-quarters of a mile below is Handley's Bridge. Here Wandale Beck enters. Half-a-mile below is High Haygarth. Here Backside Beck enters. There is also an inn. Two and three-quarter miles below High Haygarth is Hobdale Bridge. Here the Hobdale Beck enters. Law Ridding Bridge is half-a-mile below, and half-a-mile still lower Hebblethwaite Beck enters. Here is Burnt Mill Bridge, and a quarter of a mile lower Straight Bridge. The Clough River (see *ante*) enters just below Straight

Bridge. Three-quarters of a mile below Straight Bridge is Soolbank Bridge. Sedbergh stands on the right bank. Here there are inns and a railway station. A quarter of a mile below is a weir, and a quarter of a mile lower is Milnthorpe Bridge. Birks Mill and weir are about a mile below this bridge. The River Dee (see *ante*) enters a quarter of a mile lower down, and a quarter of a mile below that is the Ingleton and Tebay railway viaduct. Brig Flats is a mile below Birks Mill, and about a mile and a quarter below Brigs Flats is Marthwaite New Bridge. Here the Lancaster highway crosses. A quarter of a mile below the bridge the river enters the Lune. The whole river is a succession of streams running over a limestone bed, and on account of the high hills which surround it, is of far greater width and volume than its length suggests. The total length of the river is fifteen and a quarter miles.

RIVER RIBBLE.

The River Ribble rises at Ribblehead Spring, on Ingleton Fells, a short distance from the Richmond and Lancaster highway, and a quarter of a mile south-west of the Gearstone's Inn, one and a quarter miles from Ribblehead station. Ribblehead is 1,000 feet above sea level. The chief gathering grounds on the highest reaches of the river lie between Whernside, Ingleborough, and Cam Fell. About a quarter of a mile from its source, the Ribble receives the Gale Beck, a considerable tributary which drains the Gale Moors, and the north-west side of Cam Fell. The most important tributaries to the Ribble, which enter the river in the order named, are Cam Beck, Horton Beck, Stainforth Beck, Ings Beck, Bashall Brook, the River Hodder (an important angling stream, see *ante*), and the River Calder, the latter polluted. The country through which the Ribble runs above Settle is the limestone district, and the high rugged hills fall rapidly to the stream. The country, however, is very picturesque, as it is throughout the whole length of the river which concerns the angler. Below Settle it enters upon a flat country which continues to Cow Bridge, below Long Preston. This part of the river is known as the deeps, and holds a great quantity of coarse fish. Below Long Preston it becomes a veritable trout and salmon stream again, and thus it continues through Ribblesdale proper, until it is joined by the Calder, about a mile below Mitton Bridge, when as an angling stream it is of no further importance. It runs to the sea below Preston. The River Calder is highly polluted, and thus what would be one of the finest salmon rivers in the country is greatly discounted. The salmon can only get past the pollutions in the freshes. In the higher reaches of the river there is nothing but trout. In the deeps or middle reaches, pike and chub, and a few grayling; and in the lower reaches, salmon, sea trout, and brown trout. Salmon get as far up the river as Settle Bridge. The salmon fishing commences about the end of August, when the nets are all taken off the river.

From the source to Helwith Bridge, nine and a quarter miles, the fishing on both sides is in the hands of the Manchester Anglers' Association. Hon. secretary, Mr. Ed. R. Austin, 274, Great Clowes Street, Higher Broughton, Manchester.

The affairs of the association are managed by a committee. River watcher, Robert Walker, New Inn Bridge, Horton-in-Ribblesdale. Limited to eighty members. Entrance fee, one guinea; annual subscription, two guineas; no short period tickets are issued. The fishing is strictly preserved, and confined to members only, and outsiders have no chance of getting permission. Date of close time, October 1st to March 5th. No fish to be taken under 8in. The fishing in the tributaries on the association length also belongs to them; they have also a tarn two miles above Horton, which is well stocked with big trout; the limit in the tarn is 10in.; there is nothing but trout, and it is all first-class fishing. The best months are August and September for the Ribble, and May and June for the tarn. At Horton-in-Ribblesdale, on the Horton Beck, they have a trout breeding house, and breed twenty-eight to thirty thousand a year, with which to stock the river. The association was founded in 1878. The nearest railway station is Horton-in-Ribblesdale, six miles north of Settle. At Horton there are two inns, where accommodation may be had. There is an inn at Helwith Bridge, at the foot of the fishing, but no beds to be had. At Ribblehead there is also an inn, with sleeping rooms for three persons. Dogs not allowed. Members must produce their tickets and show the contents of their creels when challenged. No Sunday fishing. No fishing permitted before 6 a.m., nor after 9 p.m., except in June and July, when the time is extended to 10 p.m. In Newhouse Tarn no angler to kill more than four fish on one day. The association is a very enterprising one, possesses a library of angling works, and a manuscript magazine for the reception of original papers read before the association, and for communications from members in prose and verse. The association is as much social and literary as piscatorial, and preference is given to candidates for election whose residence within easy reach of Manchester will enable them to attend the monthly meetings. Gale Beck enters the Ribble a quarter of a mile below Ribblehead. Selside is three and a quarter miles below, and Cam Beck enters a quarter of a mile below Selside. New Inn Bridge is three miles below Cam Beck. Horton-in-Ribblesdale is half-a-mile below New Inn Bridge, and Helwith Bridge is two and a quarter miles below Horton. Here the Manchester Anglers' Association water ends.

The fishing below Helwith Bridge to Langwith Mill Weir (two and a half miles) belongs to Mr. Foster Knowles, of Stainforth, and is private. Stainforth Bridge is a mile and a half below Helwith Bridge. Stainforth Force is a little below the bridge, and Stainforth Beck enters a quarter of a mile below. The fishing is all private from Langcliffe Mill to Settle Bridge, except three fields on the right side of the river above Settle Bridge. These are open fishing. Stackhouse is half-a-mile below Langcliffe Weir. There is also a weir at Stackhouse. Settle Bridge is a mile below Stackhouse. Salmon do not get higher up the river than the weir at Settle Bridge. From Settle Bridge to Gas-house Bridge (about half-a-mile) Mr. Brayshaw occasionally grants permission. At Settle there are several inns, and a railway station on the Settle and Carlisle branch. Giggleswick Station, on the Skipton and Lancaster branch, is about a mile distant. For about a quarter of a mile below Gas-house Bridge, where the Settle irrigation fields come in, permission to fish can be had from the Ashfield Hotel, Settle. From the bottom of the length to Runley Beck both sides,

Mr. John Birbeck, of Anley House, occasionally grants permission. Runley Beck is about a mile below Gas-house Bridge. From Runley Beck to Mere Beck, on the left, two miles, and to New Hall, on the right, three-quarters of a mile, the fishing is private. The coarse fishing starts at Mere Beck. This is where the deeps commence. From New Hall to Rathmell Beck, on the right, permission to fish can be had from the owners or tenants. Below Mere Beck to Preston Ings, about a mile on the left bank, permission can be had from the Ashfield Hotel, Settle. Rathmell Beck is two miles below Mere Beck. From the bottom of the Ashfield length, on the left, to Cow Bridge at Long Preston, tickets to fish can be had free of charge at the Boar's Head Inn, Long Preston. Cow Bridge is a mile and a half below Rathmell Beck. There are several inns and a railway station at Long Preston. Here the coarse fishing ends. From Rathmell Beck to Cow Bridge it is private on the right.

From Cow Bridge, Long Preston, to about three-quarters of a mile below Sawley Bridge, a distance of thirteen and a half miles, the fishing on both sides is private. Mr. C. B. Wright, of Bolton Hall, and Earl Cowper, do on very rare occasions grant tickets to fish some portions of this length. Halton Bridge is two and a half miles below Cow Bridge. It is one mile to Hellifield Station and inn. Halton Place Park commences at the bridge, and ends about a mile lower down. This is Colonel Harrison's length of fishing and strictly private. Newsholme is a mile and three-quarters below Halton Bridge. There is a railway station. Paythorne Bridge is two miles below Newsholme. Gisburn Bridge is a mile and three-quarters below Paythorne Bridge. It is three-quarters of a mile from the bridge to Gisburn, where there are inns and a railway station. Bolton Hall is three miles below Gisburn Bridge. Sawley Bridge is a mile and three-quarters below Bolton Bridge. At Sawley Bridge there is an inn and a weir just above the bridge. It is two miles to Rimington Station. From Sawley Bridge to Higher Horrocksford on the left, two and a quarter miles, the fishing is private.

From three-quarters of a mile below Sawley Bridge, on the right, to Grindleton Ford, and from Higher Horrocksford, on the left, to the lower boundary of the water belonging to the Clitheroe Corporation, a little above Bungerley Bridge, the fishing is in the hands of the Clitheroe Angling Association. Chairman, Major Dewhurst; vice-chairman, Mr. C. H. Rowlandson; hon. secretary, Mr. J. L. Bulcock, Castle Street, Clitheroe; committee, Messrs. A. Sykes, G. Howard, J. J. Smithers, J. Allen, and J. Lofthouse. Entrance free, 20s. Yearly subscription fixed at each annual meeting in January. Tickets to be shown when challenged. Limit for trout, 8in. Nothing but artificial fly and natural stone-fly or creeper allowed from March 1st to June 15th, after which date any legal bait may be used until September 15th. River watchers, John Wrigley, West Bradford, near Clitheroe; and Robert Moon, Cross Street, Clitheroe. Trout and salmon fishing principally, a few grayling above Clitheroe, and a quantity of chub in some parts below. From Sawley Bridge to Smithies Bridge House it is about one mile. From here the road leads to Clitheroe, and it is one mile to Chatburn Station. A short distance below Smithies Bridge the river crosses the Yorkshire boundary into Lancashire on the left bank. Grindleton Ford is one mile and a quarter below Smithies Bridge. From this point it is half-mile to Chatburn Railway Station, and a quarter of a mile to Grindleton. Higher Horrocksford is a quarter of a mile below Grindleton Ford. From Grindleton Ford to Edisford Bridge, on the right, or Yorkshire side, the fishing is private. West Bradford Bridge and Horrocksford are half-a-mile below Grindleton Ford. From Bradford Bridge to Bungerley it is one mile. This is the bottom limit of the Clitheroe Angling Association's water, on the left or Lancashire side. Bungerley Bridge is a short quarter of a mile below. Clitheroe stands opposite, half-a-mile wide of the river. There is a railway station and numerous inns. Below the Association length comes a short piece owned by Mr. Eli Tucker, who has the refreshment establishment, and grants tickets at threepence per day. This short length is at Clitheroe, on the Lancashire side. Below, on the same side, to a little above Henthorne House, the fishing is private. There is a weir a quarter of a mile below Bungerley Bridge, and Edisford Bridge is a quarter of a mile still lower. Henthorne House is half-a-mile below Edisford Bridge. From Edisford Bridge to Hodder Foot, on the Yorkshire side, and from Henthorne House to Mitton Bridge, on the Lancashire side, the river is fishable by ticket, to be obtained free, on application at the Red Lion Inn, Clitheroe; the Three Fishes Inn, Mitton; and the Aspinall's Arms, Mitton. These tickets also embrace part of the fishing on the Hodder (see *ante*). Below Whalley, on the Lancashire side, to opposite Hodder Foot, the fishing is private, From Edisford Bridge to Mitton Bridge it is two miles and three-quarters. There is good accommodation at the inns at the latter place. It is two miles to Whalley Station. Half-a-mile below Mitton Bridge the Hodder enters the Ribble on the Yorkshire side, and the river leaves the county of York for Lancashire. About half-a-mile still lower the River Calder enters on the opposite side; the pollutions therefrom make the Ribble of little use below for angling purposes. The total length of the Ribble in Yorkshire is forty-two and three-quarter miles.

RIVER RICCALL.

The Riccall commences at Cony Birks and Carlton Park Woods, about three miles and a half north of Helmsley. The confluence of the Cowhouse and Bonfield Gill Becks form the source of the Riccall. Cowhouse Beck receives Bogmire Beck a little higher up, and the three streams conjointly drain Helmsley East Moors. The river runs through charming woods down Riccall-dale until it enters the vale of Pickering, at Riccall Bridge; thence it flows through a perfectly flat country until it enters the Lower Rye, at Salton. The best centre for the angler is Helmsley. The nearest railway stations: Hemsley, Nawton, and Nunnington.

The angling (trout and grayling) is good. The greater portion of the stream on both sides is fishable by ticket, procurable at the Earl of Feversham's Estate Office, Helmsley. Prices: for the season, which ends October 1st, 12s.; three months, 7s.; one month, 3s.; one week, 1s. Lures: artificial fly or minnow. No worm fishing allowed. Close time for trout, October 1st to March 31st. No fish to be killed under 6½in.; all baskets, if required, to be submitted to the inspection of Lord Feversham's keepers. The same rules apply to the portions which are fishable by permission from the other owners and tenants. Full particulars are distinctly set forth on the tickets. Lord Feversham's water extends down the right side from the source to just below Crook House, and down the left side from the source to the bridge from Ness to Muscoates. Below those points permission is readily granted by the owners and tenants. The top length of the river, above Riccall Bridge, runs through a succession of open glades, bordered by woods, which are very beautiful. Riccall Bridge is four and three-quarter miles from the source. Helmsley is a mile on the one hand from the bridge, and Nawton a mile and a half on the other. There are inns and railway stations at both places.

Harome is two and a quarter miles below Riccall Bridge. Here there is an inn, and it is two miles to Nunnington Station, and two and a half miles to Helmsley Station. Crook House is a mile and a quarter below Harome. This is the bottom limit of the Earl of Feversham's water on the right side. Below, permission can be had from the owners and tenants. The footbridge which leads from Ness to Muscoates is two and a quarter miles below Crook House. The bridge is the bottom limit of the Earl of Feversham's water on the left side, and below, permission to fish can be had from the owners and tenants. The Riccall enters the Rye near Salton, where there is an inn. The village is three-quarters of a mile wide of the river, the total length of which is twelve and a quarter miles. Slingsby is the nearest railway station, three miles.

RIVER ROTHER.

The River Rother has its source in Derbyshire. It joins the county of York at the point where County Dyke joins the river, about one mile south of Waleswood. For a considerable distance it forms the county boundary, and enters the county of York entirely where Beighton Mill goit tail joins the river. Thence it runs by Treeton, Catcliffe, Whiston, and Rotherham, where it joins the River Don. The Yorkshire length of the river is ten and a quarter miles, the whole of which is in a high state of pollution.

RIVER RYE.

The Rye has its source on the southern edge of the Cleveland Hills at Rye Head Spring, 1,020 feet above the sea. The highest tributaries which drain the moors under the south edge of the Cleveland Range are Stonymoor Sike, Prodale, Arndale, and Wheat Becks, the latter also gathering the waters from the north side of Black Hambleton. At Blow Gill the Blow Gill Beck enters. This stream drains the Hawnby and Snilesworth Moors. Below this point, on the west side, several streams fall from the north-east side of the Hambleton Hills, running through Eskerdale, Thorodale, and Gowerdale. At Hawnby, Ladhill Beck joins. This is another considerable tributary running from the edge of Bilsdale Moor. The most important tributary above Helmsley is the River Seph, which has its origin in the Raisdale and Bilsdale Becks, and flows down Bilsdale, receiving the Ledge Beck in its course. The River Seph was once an important angling stream, but the hush from the lead mines has killed all the fish. The river now enters the vale, and the tributaries are the Riccall (see *ante*), the Dove (see *ante*), the Hodge Beck (see *ante*), and the Costa Beck (see *ante*). The River Rye is a succession of ideal trout streams and pools until it reaches Nunnington, then it becomes deep, narrow, and sluggish, running lazily in the bottom between wide flood banks. In the lower reaches pike, chub, dace, and grayling are plentiful, but above Nunnington trout abound, and the angling is of a very high character, the Ryedale Club length being the best on the river. For details see below.

From the source to Shaken Bridge the fishing is free, but above Close Bridge the fish run very small. The rules mentioned below, and issued at the Helmsley Estate Office, must also be adhered to on the open lengths.

Prodale Beck enters the river one and a half miles below the source. Wheat Beck comes in a mile and a half below that point, and Blow Gill Beck two miles below Wheat Beck. Eskerdale Beck enters a mile below Blow Gill Beck, and all these becks hold small fish. Hawnby, where there is an inn, is eight and a half miles below the source. Helmsley is the nearest railway station. Hawnby or Ladhill Beck comes in just below. The fishing in this beck is very good, but it is strictly private. The River Seph enters a mile and a half below Hawnby. Shaken Bridge is a mile and a half below Hawnby.

From Shaken Bridge to Rievaulx Bridge, both sides, the river is fishable by ticket, obtainable at the Earl of Feversham's Estate Office, Helmsley. Season, which ends October 1st, 12s.; three months, 7s.; four weeks, 3s.; one week, 1s. Lures: Artificial fly or minnow. No worm fishing allowed. Close time for trout, October 1st to March 31st. No fish to be taken under 6½in. All baskets, if required, to be submitted to the inspection of Lord Feversham's keepers. From Shaken Bridge to Rievaulx Bridge it is three and a half miles. Helmsley is the nearest railway station to Rievaulx Bridge. From Rievaulx Bridge to Helmsley Bridge is the strictly private fishing of Lord Feversham. Rievaulx Abbey stands just above the bridge. This is one of the loveliest parts of Yorkshire. A mile and a quarter below Rievaulx Bridge the river enters Duncombe Park, and for three miles and a quarter runs through one of the most charming demesnes in the county. The park ends at Helmsley. This is a capital angling centre not only for the Rye, but for the Riccall, Dove, and Hodge, all of which are fishable by ticket from the Helmsley Estate Office. There are some very good inns at Helmsley, also a railway station. The Dale Beck enters at Helmsley Bridge, which is the end of Lord Feversham's private water, and the commencement of the Ryedale Anglers' Club length.

The Ryedale Anglers' Club length commences at Helmsley Bridge, and extends on both sides of the river to Block Plantation, which is a little below the railway bridge. This is one of the best lengths of fishing in Yorkshire, and the club one of the most exclusive. President, the Earl of Feversham, who has free transferable tickets for his personal friends. The membership is limited to twenty, annual subscription five and a half guineas, and entrance fee four guineas. Members are elected by ballot, subject to the approval of Lord Feversham, and the affairs of the club managed by a committee. Hon. secretary, Alfred Pearson, Esq., manager, Union Bank, Helmsley, *via* York. Beck watcher, John Storey, Helmsley. The fishing on this length is good all the year round. The trout run a little over the average for Yorkshire trout, and the grayling are a good size and very plentiful. Nothing but artificial fly and minnow allowed. A member may at any time, except in the month of June, take with him one friend to fish with artificial fly only, on the express stipulation that the member shall, in the strictest sense, accompany his friend. Trout fishing season, April 1st to October 1st. Grayling may be taken throughout the year. Limit for trout 8½in. Angling for salmon strictly prohibited. No member permitted to fish more than twenty-one days in any one year, and whenever a member takes a friend it shall count as two days' fishing. The head keeper sends to the secretary a weekly list of the gentlemen who have visited the stream. The keepers have power to examine panniers. From Helmsley Bridge to Block Plantation, the limits of the Ryedale Club, it is four and three-quarter miles. Harome is two miles below Helmsley Bridge and three-quarters of a mile wide of the river. Nunnington railway station is a mile and a quarter wide of the river.

From Block Plantation to Ness Bridge the fishing on both sides belongs to —. Rutson, Esq., of Newby Whiske, who occasionally grants permission to anglers to fish the length from the bottom limit of the Ryedale Club, to the White Bridge at Nunnington. Below that point he reserves the water for himself and friends—strictly private. From Block Plantation to the White Bridge at Nunnington it is a mile and a half. At Nunnington there are inns. The railway station is a mile and a half from the village. Ness

Bridge is a mile and a half below the White Bridge. From Ness Bridge to just below Salton Bridge, —. Kendal, Esq., of East Ness, grants permission to fish the river on both sides. Grayling fishing good. It is two and a half miles from Ness Bridge to Slingsby Station. The River Riccall enters the Rye a mile and a half below Ness Bridge. Salton Bridge is just below Riccall Mouth. Salton is three-quarters of a mile wide of the river. Here are two inns. Mr. Kendal's fishing ends at Low Waterholmes, below Salton Bridge.

Below Low Waterholmes, on the right, to Swinton Drain, permission to fish must be obtained from the owners or tenants. Also on the left to Rye Mouth. There is but little difficulty in getting permission so long as anglers conduct themselves properly. Grayling, pike, chub, and dace are found in the lower reaches, but very few trout below Newsham Bridge. The River Dove (see *ante*) enters on the left, a quarter of a mile below Low Waterholmes. Butterwick Bridge is a mile and three-quarters below Dove Mouth. It is two miles from the bridge to Barton-le-Street Station. Brawby, where there is an inn, is a mile and a half below Butterwick Bridge. The River Seven (see *post*) enters half-a-mile below Brawby. Newsham Bridge is a mile and a half below Brawby. It is one and a half miles from Newsham to Amotherby Station. Great Habton, where there is an inn, is half-a-mile below Newsham Bridge, and Swinton Drain is two miles below.

From Swinton Drain, on the right, to Rye Mouth, the fishing belongs to Earl Fitzwilliam. Fishing tickets are granted free on application at the Fitzwilliam Estate Offices, Old Maltongate, Malton, on which full instructions for the guidance of anglers are set forth. For details see River Derwent. On the opposite side permission to fish must be had from the tenants. Ryton Bridge is two miles below Swinton Drain, and two and three-quarter miles from Malton. Howe Bridge is three-quarters of a mile below Ryton Bridge. The highway from Malton to Pickering crosses at Howe Bridge, and the River Costa enters the Rye at the same point. This is a high-class angling stream (see *ante*). It is three and a half miles from Howe Bridge to Malton. Rye Mouth is a mile and a half below Howe Bridge. The Rye enters the River Derwent near Wykeham. Rillington is the nearest railway station to Rye Mouth, one and a half miles. The total length of the Rye is forty miles. The Board of Conservators have recently turned a quantity of yearling trout into the Rye.

"THE RYE" (No. 7 of the Yorkshire Rivers Series), with bird's-eye view of the roads and surrounding country, by Tom Bradley, being a most complete angler's or tourist's guide, showing all places of note on the banks of the river, with brief descriptions of the legends and folk lore of the district. May be obtained at the office of *The Yorkshire Post*, Leeds, or ordered through any bookseller, price 6d., by post 7½d.

SCALBY BECK.

Scalby Beck is connected with the River Derwent by means of a cut. It carries off the water from Burniston Beck and the Kirk Beck, which run through Scalby village. In flood times the volume of water it carries off from the Derwent is sometimes greater than that in the river itself. From the Derwent to Scalby Bridge the water flows through a cut which is almost a dead level. Between Scalby and Newby Bridges there is a long deep, and thence to the sea, there is a great variety of water. There are no less than eight high dams, with large pools beneath, and several smaller dams. From the lowest to the sea, the stream is fast-running over a rocky bed, with several little pools.

It is all trout fishing in Scalby Beck. There are a few big chub in one or two of the dead reaches,, but they are rarely fished for. In autumn there is a fair amount of bull trout, with an occasional sea trout. They only get about a mile up from the sea, and provide good sport. The stock of trout is constantly being replenished from the Derwent and Burniston Beck.

The whole of the water, with the exception of a few short breaks, belongs to the Scalby Angling Club. President, Dr. W. E. Everley Taylor ; hon. secretary and treasurer, Mr. J. W. Blakey, Editor, *Northern Angler*, Scarborough ; river watcher, A. Gough, Newby Mill Farm. Limited to twenty members. No short period tickets. A friend may accompany a member, who can allow him to use his rod. Close time, October 22nd to March 15th. Limit of takeable fish, 8in. No minnow fishing except in July and August. The intervals in the club water are the small field in which Scalby Cottage stands, on the south bank near the sea ; the dead stretch between the bridges at Scalby village ; and a field on the north side where Wilkinson's Mill stands, which is owned by a club of the same name, and lets out day tickets at 2s. Visitors using these tickets are cautioned against trespassing on the Scalby Club waters.

The point at which the Scalby Cut leaves the Derwent is 140 feet above the sea. Scalby is about three miles from the Derwent. This is the length which is almost dead level. Then the best part of the stream commences, and begins to fall very rapidly. There are inns and a railway station at Scalby, which is on the Scarborough and Whitby branch of the North Eastern Railway. Newby Bridge is just below Scalby, and Burniston Beck (see *ante*), a good angling stream, also enters on the low side of the village. The total length of Scalby Beck, from the Derwent to the sea, is four miles and three-quarters. The beck enters the sea at Scalby Ness Point, two miles north of Scarborough.

RIVER SEVEN.

The River Seven rises 1,300 feet above sea level at Rosedale Head, on the south side of Westerdale Moor, and about a mile from the source of the River Esk. It runs from the moors down Rosedale, draining in the upper reaches the east side of Farndale Moor and the west side of Rosedale Common. At Rosedale Abbey the river receives its first important tributary in Northdale Beck, which runs down Northdale from Rosedale Common. Below Rosedale Abbey the river drains the east side of Spaunton Moor and Hartoft Moor, receiving Hartoft Beck at Hartoft End. It afterwards runs down the dale through Sinnington, Marton, and Normanby to the Rye. Below Sinnington the stream runs through a comparatively flat country, and below Normanby through a dead level country, the river being somewhat sluggish in its lowest reaches and bordered with high flood banks. It rises very rapidly in flood times. From Rosedale to Hartoft Bridge it is a succession of rocky streams. Below the junction of Hartoft Beck it becomes a good sized stream. The owners on the whole length of the stream keep the fishing for themselves and friends, from whom permission to fish must be obtained. On some lengths of the stream it is not difficult for visitors to obtain permission. The fish at the source are similar to moor trout. Below the junction of Hartoft Beck there is two miles of good fishing to Askew Bridge. At Appleton Farm and Mill, and below almost to Sinnington, the water is strictly preserved. This is the best fishing on the Seven. Nothing but trout, which run a good size. The owners grant occasional tickets to fish this water. Limit, 8in. At Sinnington and below the fish are large in size, particularly in the mill dam and pools. Trout over 1lb., and chub much larger. Good fishing below down to Marton, "the Garden of Ryedale." No coarse fish above Sinnington. A small quantity of chub below. As the stream gets into the flat country jack pike, 2lb. chub, and grayling from $\frac{1}{2}$lb. to $1\frac{1}{2}$lb. are found. Thorgill Bridge is four and a quarter miles below the source. Dun Carr Bridge half-a-mile still lower. A mile below Dun Carr Bridge are Bow Bridge and Rosedale Abbey. Here there is an inn. Hartoft Bridge is three-quarters of a mile lower down. Here Hartoft Beck enters. This beck is good fishing after a fresh. Askew Bridge is two miles lower down. Half-a-mile below Askew Bridge Cropton Beck enters. There is a weir. Cropton stands half-a-mile wide of the river. Here there is an inn. Appleton Mill and weirs are three-quarters of a mile below. Sinnington Bridge is two miles and a half lower still. At Sinnington there is an inn. It is three miles to Kirbymoorside. This is the best centre. Sinnington Grange is two miles below Sinnington Bridge. A bridge and weir at this point. Catter Beck enters just below. Marton Bridge is three miles below Sinnington Bridge. Inn at Marton. Normanby Bridge (inn) is a mile and a half below Marton Bridge. Barugh Bridge is two miles lower down, and Brawby a mile still lower. Inns at both places. Three-quarters of a mile below Brawby the River Seven enters the Rye at Little Habton. The total length of the stream is twenty-two and three-quarter miles.

RIVER SKELL.

The River Skell rises at Skell Grains, on the Pateley Moors, 1,110 feet above the sea, and runs to the Ure below Ripon. For the first two miles of its course it runs through high moorlands, and is a mere mountain stream without tributaries, the only tributary of importance in the whole length being the River Laver. The Skell runs through Grantley Park, and the grounds of Fountains Abbey and Studley Royal. At the latter place it is carried through two small lakes, and by the aid of a canal feeds several ornamental ponds in the grounds. Within Grantley Park there is also a lake. These lakes and ponds all contain fish, but are in the private hands of Lord Grantley and the Marquis of Ripon, as is the whole of the fishing in the Skell above Hell Wath. Below Hell Wath it belongs to the Ripon Angling Club. The fishing is first-class in the whole of the river. There is nothing but trout, except in the bottom half-mile : that length holds a good many grayling.

High Grantley is six miles from the source of the river. Here there is an inn and the Skell enters the Grantley Hall grounds. At two miles above High Grantley a stream from the High Fish Pond enters the river. These both hold good fish. Grantley Hall is just below the village. The lake in Grantley Park is about half-a-mile below the village. Sawley is two and a half miles below High Grantley. Fountains Bridge is a quarter of a mile below Sawley. Here the Skell enters Fountains Abbey grounds. Fountains Abbey is half-a-mile below Sawley. The river enters Studley Park half-a-mile below the Abbey ; also the small lake at the bottom of which the canal commences which feeds the ponds. The canal falls into the large lake one mile below the Abbey. All these ponds and lakes hold fish. The fishing is strictly private. The river leaves Studley Park two miles below the Abbey. Hell Wath is a mile and a quarter lower down.

At Hell Wath the Ripon Angling Club water commences, and extends to the Ure—both sides—without a break. The club has also lengths of water on the Ure and Laver. Hon. secretary and treasurer, Arthur J. H. Wood, Esq., Bellwood, Ripon. The water on the Skell from Hell Wath to Borrage Bridge is reserved strictly for the use of the club members. The secretary has power to grant free tickets for the water, which extends from Borrage Bridge to the Ure, to persons residing within a radius of two miles of Ripon. Any angler outside this limit is charged one shilling and sixpence per day. This ticket also allows him to fish in the club's water in the Ure. For further details see the Ure and the Laver.

Bishopton is half-a-mile below Hell Wath and a quarter of a mile wide of the river. The River Laver enters on the left, just below Bishopton Mills (see *ante*). Borrage Bridge, Ripon, is one mile below Hell Wath. Several inns. Three-quarters of a mile to the railway station. A mile below Borrage Bridge the Skell joins the Ure half-a-mile above Hewick Bridge. The length of the Skell from source to mouth is fourteen and a half miles.

RIVER SKIRFARE.

The River Skirfare is an important tributary of the Wharfe. It is only called Skirfare below Arncliffe ; above that place it is a succession of becks under various names. The first is called Foxup Beck, which rises at Foxup Beck Spring on Foxup Moor, Pennegent side, 1,470 feet above the sea. From Cush Beck to Litton the stream is called Halton Gill Beck. Below Litton it is called Broad Beck to Arncliffe, where it becomes the Skirfare.

The best of the fishing (all trout), which is most excellent, belongs to the club (for particulars see River Wharfe). But there is some very good fishing above Hawkswick, the angling on both sides being in the hands of the owners and tenants, from whom permission must be obtained. The principal of these is Mr. James Hammond. Permission to fish can also be had at the Falcon Hotel, Arncliffe. The fishing is little good above Litton. Skipton is the nearest railway station, to and from which place the mail-cart carries passengers.

The places *en route* from the source are Foxup (one and three-quarter miles), Halton Gill (two and a half miles), Hesleden (four miles), and Litton (five miles). At Litton there is an inn, and a footpath across Birks Fell to Buckden (four miles).

Arncliffe Bridge is two and a half miles below Litton. From the bridge there is a footpath across Hawkswick Moor to Kettlewell (two and a half miles). Arncliffe stands on the right bank. Two miles below is Hawkswick, on the left bank. Here the Kilnsey Club length commences, and extends on both sides to the Wharfe. The total length of the Skirfare is eleven and a half miles, the Kilnsey Club length about two miles. About half-a-mile above the junction with the Wharfe is Skirfare Bridge, from which there is a highway to Kettlewell (two and a quarter miles) and to Kilnsey (three-quarters of a mile). There are inns at both places. Kilnsey is thirteen miles from Skipton, which is the nearest railway station. The mail-cart carries passengers.

RIVER SWALE.

The source of the River Swale is formed by the confluence of the Great Sleddale and Birkdale Becks near Stonehouse Bridge, about two and a half miles above Keld. Great Sleddale Beck has its source near that of the River Ure, rising a short distance away on the other side of the mountain. Sleddale is a flat moorland valley a few miles in length, which slopes gently from the very summit of the mountains. This stream gathers the waters that fall from Great Shunner Fell, 2,344 feet above sea level, and Angram Common on the one hand and Burnt Moor on the other. Wavery Gill and Blackberry Becks drain into it. Birkdale Beck, which is a continuation of Little Sleddale Beck, runs through a wild mountainous ravine, its chief gathering grounds being Little Sleddale, Lodge Side, Uldale Gill, and Coldberg Edge. These streams are of considerable length and volume, and hold plenty of small trout. The nearest railway station is Kirkby Stephen, eight miles. There is nothing but trout in the higher reaches of the Swale, which run through a wild mountainous district. The tributaries are numerous, and many of them of importance as angling streams. Whitsundale Beck enters the river one mile below its source. This beck, which runs from Ravenseat Moor, holds plenty of small trout. Low Bridge is half-a-mile below Whitsundale Beck, and Park Bridge half-a-mile still lower. Weststonedale enters just below Park Bridge. This beck receives the Eaststonedale Beck, both becks draining the Stonedales Moor. The fishing in these becks is no good except after a fresh. Keld is half-a-mile below Park Bridge. From Keld the Swale winds round the foot of Kisdon mountain to Muker. It runs down a steep craggy glen, thickly crowded with underwood, and shut in by high mountains. Kisdon Force is a quarter of a mile below Keld. There is an inn at Keld, which is the highest village in the dale. Swinner Gill Beck enters a mile below Keld. The fishing in this stream is only poor. Ramp's Holme Bridge is a mile and a quarter below Swinner Gill, and Muker is half-a-mile still lower.

Muker is the best centre for fishing the top end of Swaledale. Here there are two inns, and it is seven miles to Hawes, which is the nearest railway station. Muker Beck enters on the low side of the village. This beck, which is about one and a half miles long, runs round the other side of Kisdon mountain from the village of Thwaite, and is formed by Thwaite Beck and Cliffe Beck. There is some fair trout fishing in this stream. From Muker the river runs down a beautiful dale to Richmond. It gradually begins to widen out, and between Feetham and Healaugh it has the same wide beds of shingle that characterise it below Catterick Bridge. From the source of the River Swale to its junction with Arkle Beck at Grinton Bridge, the fishing rights in the river and its tributaries belong to Captain Lyell, the lord of the manors of Muker and Healaugh, with the exception of those over half the bed of the stream, from Isles Bridge to Grinton Bridge on the south side of the river, which are also private. Most of these fishing rights are let to the tenants of the grouse moors, and in the majority of cases permission to fish is not difficult to obtain. There is some good trouting, but the river below Gunnerside suffers materially from the hush from the lead mines. A mile and a quarter below Muker is Ivelet Bridge. A little above the bridge Mill Beck enters. This beck, which is preserved, holds some good trout. Leave is occasionally granted. Ivelet Beck enters just below the bridge. It holds a few small trout. A mile below Ivelet Bridge is Gunnerside Bridge. There are inns at Gunnerside, and here the Gunnerside Beck enters. This beck runs from Gunnerside Moors, and is almost ruined by the hush from the lead mines on those moors. Two miles below Gunnerside Bridge is Isles Bridge. Here the Crackpot Beck enters. This is a fair trout stream, but private. Low Row is half-a-mile below Isles Bridge, and Feetham another half-mile still lower. There is an inn at Feetham. Two miles below Feetham is Healaugh. Just above the hamlet Healaugh Beck enters. This beck for angling purposes is almost ruined by the hush from the lead mines. Two miles below Healaugh, Arkle Beck enters the Swale (see *ante*). Reeth stands on this beck half-a-mile wide of the river. A quarter of a mile below the beck mouth is Grinton Bridge. Here the Grinton Beck enters, and it is six miles to Redmire in Wensleydale, which is the nearest railway station. It is half-a-mile to Reeth, which is the best centre for fishing this part of Swaledale and Arkle Beck. There is good accommodation. A conveyance runs once a day between Reeth and Richmond.

Below Grinton the river runs through green pastures past Ellerton Priory until it enters the deep falling woods of Stainton Spring, continuing through some beautiful and striking scenery to Downholme Bridge and Marske, tumbling over a rocky limestone bed with huge moss-grown boulders thrown up in its midst. The fishing in this part of the river—that is, from Grinton to Marske Beck end—is private. Marrick Priory is a mile and three-quarters below Grinton Bridge. Ellerton Priory is three-quarters of a mile lower down. Two miles below Ellerton Priory Downholme stands half-a-mile wide of the river. Here there are inns. Two and three-quarter miles below Ellerton Priory is Downholme Bridge. From the bridge it is one mile to Marske, where there is an inn. Marske Beck enters about half-a-mile below the bridge. This is a good trout stream, but the fishing is private, leave being occasionally granted.

From Marske the river runs through a charming vale, hemmed in by high hills, to Richmond. It is a succession of streams and pools, and, about Lownethwaite Bridge, running through broad beds of shingle. From Marske Beck end to Richmond the tenants grant permission to fish readily enough, in fact, little or nothing is said so long as anglers conduct themselves like sportsmen.

Lownethwaite Bridge is three miles below Marske Beck end. Hudswell, where there is an inn, stands a little wide of the bridge. Two miles below Lownethwaite Bridge is Richmond High Bridge. From the source of the river to Richmond the highway runs through the valley and clings to the stream the whole distance, with the exception of a few miles, where it winds round Kisdon Hill from Keld to Muker. Richmond is the highest railway station in the dale, and at that town there is plenty of good accommodation.

Below Richmond the nature of the country through which the Swale runs quickly changes, and, after leaving the sylvan glades about Easby Abbey, it enters upon a flat country, which extends the whole of its remaining course, till it joins the Ure in forming the Ouse. There are plenty of nice streams, however, until considerably below Catterick Bridge. The peculiar features of the river from Catterick Bridge to Langton are the irregularities of the current, which threads its serpentine course through numerous beds of gravel and shingle, washed up by the floods, and left high and dry by the shifting nature of the stream. Below Langton the deeps commence, and the slow-running character of the river increases as it winds past Morton, Pickhill, Skipton Bridge, Topcliffe, and Brafferton, all noted angling resorts. The lower reaches of the river are slow and sluggish, with deep sedgy banks much overgrown with willows. Below Richmond there are plenty of grayling and trout, and below Langton the fishing is confined to coarse fish, with an occasional trout. The coarse fishing in the lower reaches is good ; pike, chub, roach, dace, perch, and eels, the best of the coarse fishing being about Skipton Bridge and Brafferton. From Richmond to Catterick Bridge permission to fish must be had from the owners or tenants. Richmond railway bridge is half-a-mile below the High Bridge. There is a weir just above the railway bridge. Easby Abbey is a mile below Richmond. Two and three-quarter miles below Easby is Brompton-upon-Swale. Here there are inns. One mile below Brompton is Catterick Bridge. Here there are inns and a railway station. It is one and a quarter miles to Catterick village. The Great North Road crosses the river at this point.

From Catterick Bridge to Morton Bridge, the fishing is private. One mile below Catterick is the road to Scorton and Bolton-on-Swale, which stand three-quarters of a mile wide of the river. North Ellerton is one mile lower down, and South Ellerton a mile lower still. Langton is seven miles below Catterick Bridge. Scruton and Thirntoft are four miles below Langton. The Bedale branch railway crosses the river a mile and a half below Thirntoft, and Morton Bridge is a quarter of a mile lower down. It is three-quarters of a mile from the bridge to Ainderby Station. There are inns at Morton and Ainderby.

From Morton Bridge to the mouth of the Swale it is practically open fishing, except where private grounds and parks intervene. The farmers readily grant permission ; in fact, in most cases anglers are not molested so long as they conduct themselves properly. Gatenby is three and a quarter miles below Morton Bridge. Two and three-quarter miles below Gatenby is Allerthorpe Hall wide of the river. Maunby Ferry is four miles below Gatenby. Maunby is a quarter of a mile lower down. The Leeds and Northern Railway Bridge crosses just above the village, where there are inns. It is two miles to Newby Wiske Station. Pickhill is two and a half miles below Maunby, and three-quarters of a mile wide of the river. Here there are inns and a railway station. The coarse fishing is good here. A mile and a quarter below Pickhill the River Wiske enters (see *post*). Kirkby Wiske, where there are inns, stands one mile wide of the river. Holme is a mile below Wiske Mouth. Here there is an inn, and it is two miles to Sinderby Station. A mile and a half below Holme is Howe, from which it is three-quarters of a mile to Ainderby Quernhowe, where there is an inn, and two miles to Sinderby Station. Three-quarters of a mile below Howe is Skipton Bridge. This is a famous angling resort, aad many of the Yorkshire fishing matches are fished here. Skipton-upon-Swale stands on the left bank, and Baldersby is one mile from the bridge. There is a station at Baldersby, and inns at both places. The railway bridge is just above Catton, which is a mile below Skipton Bridge. From Catton it is a mile and a quarter to Topcliffe Station. Baldersby Park commences on the right bank a mile and a quarter below

Catton, and extends a mile down stream. Topcliffe Bridge is three miles below Catton. Their is a weir above the bridge. Topcliffe stands on the left bank, and Assenby on the right. There are inns at both places, and it is two miles and a quarter to Topcliffe Station. There is good coarse fishing at Topcliffe. A mile and a half below Topcliffe Bridge, Codbeck enters (see *ante*). Cundall, where there is an inn, is a mile and a half below Codbeck end. Thornton Bridge is two miles lower down. From the bridge it is half-a-mile to Brafferton Station. Brafferton is a mile below Thornton Bridge. This is a well-known angling resort. Several inns and a railway station. Two miles and a half below Brafferton is Myton Grange. Opposite the park the fishing is private. Myton Ferry Bridge is three-quarters of a mile below the Grange. Myton-upon-Swale, where there is an inn, stands on the left bank. It is three miles to Boroughbridge Station. Swale Nab is three-quarters of a mile below Myton. Here the Swale and the Ure join, and form the River Ouse. The total length of the River Swale is seventy-two and a half miles. The Board of Conservators have recently turned a quantity of yearling trout into this river at Richmond.

RIVER TEES.

The River Tees rises at Tees Head, 2,901 feet above sea level, on the east side, and near the summit of Cross Fell, one of the highest mountains of the Penine Range. The chief gathering grounds in the upper reaches are Milburn Forest, the sides of Scordale Head, and Mickle Fell, and Harthope, Swinehope, and

Westonhope Commons. Trout Beck, the first tributary of importance, also drains the mountainous district abutting on Milburn Forest. Below the junction of Trout Beck the Tees receives, on the left side, numerous tributaries which run from Herdship Fell, Hardwood Common, Backside Fell, and Widdyside Fell, and on the right side numerous tributaries which run from the mountainous districts north of Dufton Fell. Before it reaches Caldron Snout, the Tees spreads out into a long, irregular sheet of water, called the Weel. At Caldron Snout the river falls over the Whin Rock into the bed beneath, forming a huge broad waterfall 200 feet high. Immediately below Caldron Snout the Maize Beck (see *ante*) joins the Tees. This beck forms the county boundary, and the remainder of the Tees, from the junction of Maize Beck to the sea, forms the boundary between the counties of Yorkshire and Durham, thus it will be seen that the river belongs equally to those two counties. Below Caldron Snout to High Force the river is shallow and wide-spreading, a succession of streams running over a cobbly bottom. From Maize Beck to Middleton-in-Teesdale it receives several important tributaries, which, on the north, drain the Middleton Fells, and on the south Cronkley Fell, Holwick Fell, and Crossthwaite Fell. High Force is above Middleton. This is another high waterfall over which the river drops a distance of about 70 feet, and is very fine. Below this fall the river is a swift-running stream over a somewhat rocky bed, with hugh boulders thrown up in its midst. Below High Force to Croft the country through which the river runs is very fine all the way, particularly about Cotherstone, Lartington, Egglestone, Rokeby, and Barnard Castle. The principal tributaries that enter below High Force are the River Lune, River Balder, Grand Beck, Deepdale Beck, River Greta, Clow Beck, River Skern, Staindale Beck, and the Riven Leven. For particulars of these rivers see *ante*. The Tees is navigable to Yarm. Ordinary tides flow to High Worsall. The fishing is first-class throughout, except in the lowest reaches of the river. The salmon and bull trout do not get above High Force. Nothing but trout above that place. Nearly the whole of the tributaries hold fish. The river holds trout right away to the top, but they begin to run small above the Weel.

The top portion of the river, from the source to Maize Beck, on the Yorkshire side, is private. On the Durham side the same length is fishable by ticket procurable from Lord Barnard's agent, Mr. W. T. Scarth, Raby Castle, Staindrop. This ticket can be had free on application. Mr. John Cottman, High Force Hotel, can also give these fishing tickets free, daily or monthly, to parties staying at the hotel. Lord Barnard has about seventeen miles of fishing on the Tees. This ticket also allows the holder to fish other lengths of the river set forth below. The ticket must be returned at the expiration of the season, accompanied by stamped address. Season ends October 1st. No fishing allowed before 6 a.m. or after 9 p.m. June and July, 10 p.m. No worm or bait allowed except in clear water. Any infringement of these rules will cancel the ticket. Trout Beck, which holds fish, enters four and a quarter miles below the source. Five miles below is Dead Crook. From this point to Caldron Snout, which is two and a quarter miles below, is some of the best fishing on the river. The broad pool, known as the Weel, commences at Caldron Snout, and runs for about a mile up stream. The Weel holds some very large trout. Maize Beck enters just below Caldron Snout. Harwood Beck enters three miles and a half below Maize Beck. Harwood Beck receives Langdon Beck, and they drain conjointly Herdship Fell, Grasshill Common, and Langdon Common. Above the junction of the two becks is Langdon Beck Hotel, which is seven miles from Middleton-in-Teesdale Station. The landlord, Mr. J. C. Barker, grants tickets to fish Maize Beck, Harwood Beck, and Langdon Beck.

From the Maize Beck to the West Stotley, on the Durham side, Lord Barnard's tickets allow the holder to fish, subject to the above rules, the whole way, with the exception of a few fields about Dent Banks, where permission may also be had. On the Yorkshire side, from Maize Beck to Park End, the water is the private fishing of Lord Strathmore. Below Park End, on the same side, to Mickleton, his lordship grants from 100 to 150 tickets free, through his agent, Mr. John Brown, Bow Bank, Middleton-in-Teesdale. Cronkley Bridge is a quarter of a mile below Harwood Beck. Two miles below Cronkley Bridge is High Force. Tickets as above at the hotel. Salmon and bull trout do not get above here. There is accommodation at the hotel, and a conveyance meets all trains at Middleton Station, which is the highest station in the dale, and five miles from High Force. The trout fishing from Caldron Snout to High Force is first-class. Low Force is a mile and three-quarters below High Force, and Winch Bridge is a quarter of a mile lower down. Park End is two and a quarter miles below Winch Bridge. Dent Banks is a quarter of a mile lower down. A mile and a quarter below Dent Banks is Middleton Bridge. There is a railway station and several inns at Middleton-in-Teesdale. The River Lune (see *ante*) enters a mile and a half below Middleton Bridge. Opposite Lune Foot is West Stotley. Mickleton is a mile and a quarter below Lune Foot. Here there is an inn and railway station.

Below Mickleton, on the same side to Croft Yoke Scar, the fishing is private. From West Stotley to Burn Beck, on the Durham side, T. Hutchinson, Esq., of Egglestone Abbey, grants tickets through his agent, Mr. Thomas Hill, to fish for trout only; also another short length of water below Shipley Woods. Anglers holding these tickets are cautioned against trespassing on the length of river between Burn Beck and Shipley Woods. This is Mr. Hutchinson's private fishing. All persons found fishing without a ticket will be prosecuted. No dogs allowed. The ticket must be produced when asked for by the keepers. No fish to be taken under 6½in. Season commences February 1st, ends October 31st. Burn Beck and Croft Yoke Scar are a mile below Mickleton. From here to Balder Foot, opposite which is Shipley Woods, the river is private on both sides. Egglestone Bridge is half-a-mile below Croft Yoke Scar. Romaldkirk, where there are inns and a railway station, is three-quarters of a mile from the bridge. Balder Foot is two and three-quarter miles below Egglestone Bridge. From Balder Foot to a little below Cotherstone, is a length on both sides, fishable by ticket as above, from Mr. Hutchinson's agent. For River Balder see *ante*.

From a little below Cotherstone the fishing on the Durham side of the river down to the weir, opposite Egglestone Abbey, is embraced in Lord Barnard's ticket (see page 100). On the

Yorkshire side, from a little below Cotherstone to Barnard Castle, season tickets to fish can be had free for stamped envelope on application to the Rev. Monsignor Witham, Lartington Hall, Darlington. River watchers, Sergt. Shield, Startforth, Barnard Castle. Close time, October 2nd to February 1st, both inclusive. Trout under 7in. to be returned. Any legal tackle and bait allowed. Trout, salmon, and bull trout late in the season. No chub or grayling on this length. Good accommodation at the Fox and Hounds, Cotherstone, where details about the fishing can be had. Cotherstone is just below Balder Foot. Here there is a railway station. The Tees Valley Railway Bridge crosses the river two and a half miles below Balder Foot. One mile below this railway bridge is Deepdale Bridge. Deepdale Beck, a private trout stream, enters just above the bridge. From the bridge it is two miles to Lartington. Barnard Castle Bridge is a quarter of a mile below Deepdale Bridge. Barnard Castle is a good centre for fishing the Tees. There is good accommodation and a railway station. Mr. G. B. Richardson, fishing tackle dealer, the Teesdale Sportsman's Depôt, Barnard Castle, knows the river well, and is glad to give anglers every information (see page 159). From Barnard Castle to the weir opposite Egglestone Abbey, it is a mile and a half.

From Barnard Castle Bridge, on the Yorkshire side, to the River Greta, the fishing belongs to Mrs. Morritt, of Rokeby, who grants a limited number of tickets through her agent, Mr. James Archer, Rokeby Grove, Barnard Castle. These tickets are also occasionally granted to visitors at Mrs. Ward's, the Morritt's Arms. On the Durham side, below Egglestone weir and opposite Greta Foot, Lord Strathmore's agent grants tickets (see above). Startforth is a quarter of a mile below Barnard Castle Bridge, and Egglestone Abbey weir is a mile and a half below that bridge. The Abbey Bridge is a quarter of a mile below the weir, and Greta Foot is a mile and a quarter below Abbey Bridge. For River Greta see *ante*.

From Greta Foot the fishing on both sides down to Merrybent Railway Bridge is private, with the exception of a short length below Gainford village on the Durham side, tickets to fish which can be had from Mr. Foster, Holme Cottage, Gainford, price 1s. Whorlton Bridge is a mile and a half below Greta Foot. There is a fish weir just below the bridge. Three-quarters of a mile below Whorlton Bridge is Wycliffe. There is a ferry opposite Wycliffe Grange. Ovington is a mile below Wycliffe. Winston Bridge is a mile and a quarter below Ovington. It is one mile from the bridge to Winston railway station. A mile below Winston Bridge, the Darlington and Barnard Castle Railway crosses the river. A quarter of a mile below this railway bridge on the Durham side, the Alwent or Grand Beck enters. This is a capital little trout stream, but strictly private. A mile below the above railway bridge the line recrosses the river, and half-a-mile lower is Gainford. Here there is a railway station. Merrybent Railway Bridge is three-quarters of a mile below Gainford.

From Merrybent Railway Bridge to Piercebridge the fishing on the Durham side is private, and on the Yorkshire side it is the water of the Darlington Silver Trout Anglers' Association. President, Mr. C. H. Sharp; vice-president, Mr. Jas. Timms; treasurer, Mr. Thos. N. Lloyd; secretary, Mr. Joseph F. Smythe, fishing tackle dealer, Blackwellgate, Darlington. Membership unlimited. Entrance fee, 5s., quarterly subscription, 2s. 6d.; day tickets for outsiders, 6d., on application to the secretary. All legal baits permissible. No dogs allowed. Any member may ask an angler for his ticket on producing his own. Cliffe Hall is two miles below Merrybent Railway Bridge. There is a weir about a quarter of a mile above Cliffe Hall. Piercebridge is a quarter of a mile below Cliffe Hall. At Piercebridge the Great North Road from London to Edinburgh crosses the river. There is an inn, also a railway station.

On the Yorkshire side the water of the Silver Trout Anglers' Association extends still lower, to Clow Beck, near Croft, but Colonel Wilson, of Cliffe Hall, gives leave to labourers and workmen in the district, who can furnish him with a reference, to fish that part of the river extending from Cliffe or Piercebridge to Howden Hill Scar. These tickets are limited, and Mr. Lancaster, of the George Inn, Piercebridge, is also in receipt of a limited number for the use of visitors staying at his house, to fish the same length of water. Close time October 1st to March 31st. No artificial minnow or bottom fishing allowed. River watcher, R. Macdonald, Manfield.

On the Durham side, from Piercebridge to Ulnaby Beck, the fishing is embraced in Lord Barnard's fishing ticket (see page 100), and below comes a short length of private water which extends to the top jetty. From this jetty to Low Coniscliffe the water is in the hands of the Darlington Club, then the water is private to the low side of Nag's Head. From the low side of Nag's Head to the River Skerne the water is rented by the Silver Trout Anglers' Association. There is a weir just below Piercebridge. High Coniscliffe is one mile below Piercebridge. Ulnaby Beck is a quarter of a mile below High Coniscliffe. The top jetty is a quarter of a mile below Ulnaby Beck, and Howden Hill Scar is three-quarters of a mile lower down. From this point it is three-quarters of a mile to Manfield, where there is an inn. Cleasby is one mile below Howden Hill Scar. Low Coniscliffe stands on the opposite bank, on the Durham side. Baydale Beck is half-a-mile below Low Coniscliffe. Blackwell Bridge is two and three-quarter miles below Cleasby. From Blackwell it is one and three-quarter miles to Darlington. Stapleton, where there is an inn, is half-a-mile below Blackwell Bridge. Nag's Head is a mile and a half below Stapleton. Clow Beck is half-a-mile below Nag's Head, on the Yorkshire side. This beck is a first-class private trout stream. The River Skerne, on the Durham side, is three-quarters of a mile below Clow Beck. The fishing in the Skerne is in the hands of the Silver Trout Anglers' Association and the tenants, who readily grant permission to outsiders. The stream, which is slow-running, is confined chiefly to coarse fish, pike, chub, roach, and eels. It also holds a few large trout.

Croft Bridge is just below Skerne Mouth. Between Skerne Mouth and the bridge on the Durham side there is a short length of open fishing; then below, on the same side, the fishing is private to Bolton Park Wood. On the Yorkshire side, from Clow Beck to Spa Beck, below Croft, where the York and Newcastle Railway Bridge crosses the river, tickets to fish this water for the season can be had from Sir William Chaytor's agent, Mr. Thomas

Snaith, Croft, price 1s.; river watcher, Inspector Mabon, Blackwell. Close time, October 1st to March 31st. Fair trout fishing, also salmon, grayling, dace, chub, and a few odd pike and eels. Below Spa Beck, on the Yorkshire side, the fishing is private to opposite Bolton Park Wood. At Croft there are inns and a railway station. Spa Beck enters a quarter of a mile below Croft Bridge. Dalton, where there is an inn, is a mile and a quarter below Croft Bridge. Hurworth Bridge is two and a half miles below Dalton. There are inns at Hurworth, and it is one mile to Croft Station. Neasham is two miles below Hurworth. Here there is a ferry. Staindale Bridge is five miles below Neasham. Sockburn Hall is just below the bridge. Girsby is a mile and a quarter below Staindale Bridge, and Bolton Park Wood is half-a-mile below Girsby on the opposite side.

From opposite Bolton Park Wood to about two hundred yards below Dinsdale Dam, on the Yorkshire side, the fishing is private. On the Durham side, from Bolton Park Wood to three fields above Middleton-one-Row, the salmon and trout fishing is private, but permission can be had for the coarse fishing from the owners, Messrs. Surtees, Manor House, Dinsdale. The fishing, from the three fields above Middleton-one-Row, is taken by the Silver Trout Anglers' Association. Opposite the village of Middleton-one-Row the fishing is free, and below the village the Silver Trout Club starts again, and goes to about one mile below the village. From this point—the bottom limit of the Silver Trout Club—to Bole Hole Wood on the Durham side, and from two hundred yards below Dinsdale Dam to Bells Wood, on the Yorkshire side, the fishing is rented by Mr. John Bone, Fox and Hounds, Neasham, Darlington, who issues tickets—salmon (rod-fishing), limited to ten, £2 2s. the season; trout, unlimited, 10s. the season, monthly 5s., weekly 2s. 6d., daily 1s. These tickets can also be obtained from Mr. Rutherford, Devonport Hotel, Middleton-one Row. River watchers, Inspector Mabon and T. Wall, Fighting Cocks. No Sunday fishing. All legitimate baits allowed. Close time in accordance with the Fishery Board. This is the best salmon fishing on the river in the autumn, and should be good spring fishing now that the shackel nets are done away with. The average weight of the salmon is about ten pounds. There are also salmon trout, trout, grayling, and coarse fish. The trout run to a good size. The best time for trout fishing and spinning for salmon is March to the end of June. Bells Wood and Bole Hole, two famous pools, are the best spring salmon casts. Both are a little above the tideway. Craggy, Horney, Jack's Bushes, and Ward's streams are the best back-end salmon casts. Trout and grayling all over. Dace are numerous, also chub, which run large, and a few roach and perch. Plenty of eels. Mr. H. Feargrieve, a local angler of repute, knows the river well, and is pleased to afford anglers every information. Dinsdale Dam is three-quarters of a mile below Bolton Park Wood. There are ferries both above and below the dam. The fish lock here is very imperfect, but is to be reconstructed, otherwise the salmon fishing would be much better above. Dinsdale Bridge is a mile and a quarter below Dinsdale Dam. Middleton-one-Row is a mile below Dinsdale Bridge. Two miles and a half below Middleton-one-Row is Bole Hole Wood, and half-a-mile lower down is Bells Wood. At Middleton-one-Row and Blackwell there are fish-breeding establishments under the management of the Inspector. Fifty thousand trout ova were placed in these hatcheries this season and will be added to the river.

From the top side of Bole Hole Wood to opposite Yarm Church, on the Durham side, and from the ford on the low side of Bell's Wood to Mr. Waldy's wind pump at Low Worsall, on the Yorkshire side, is the water of the Stockton Angling Association. Limited to one hundred members. President, Mr. Jos. Bentley; vice-president, Wm. Derbyshire; secretary, R. Readman, Stockton. Entrance fee, 5s.; weekly subscription, 3d.; honorary members, 10s. 6d. per year; persons over eighteen and under twenty-one, entrance, 2s. 6d., and 2d. per week contribution. The club let out salmon tickets for the season on application to the secretary, 7s. 6d. prepaid. No dogs allowed. Limit for trout and coarse fish, 6in; pike, 12in. Close time for trout, October 1st to March 1st. Worsall Gill Wood is a mile below Bell's Wood. The ordinary tides flow to this point, but there is no salt water above Yarm as the tide merely backs up the fresh water. Low Worsall is two miles below Worsall Gill Wood, and a quarter of a mile lower down is the stream that forms the boundary of the club fishing. The Stockton Angling Association also have a few miles of Thorp Beck, a rather small tributary of the Tees, about four miles from Stockton. This is good fishing and the association have recently added 3,000 very fine and healthy young trout. From this stream to Yarm Bridge, on the Yorkshire side, and from Nelly Burdon's Beck to opposite Eaglescliffe Station, on the Durham side, Mr. George Goldie, of the hotel, Yarm, is the lessee of the fisheries. The lessee grants permission to the Stockton Club to fish from Nelly Burdon's Beck to opposite Leven Foot, on the Durham side; he also grants permission to fish to outsiders calling at his house. From Yarm Bridge to the River Leven, on the Yorkshire side, the fishing is private. Plenty of coarse fish besides salmon, trout, and grayling. Close time from October 1st to March 31st, except for coarse fish. Aislaby is two miles below Low Worsall. Yarm Bridge is a mile and a quarter lower down. Here there are inns and a railway station. Nelly Burdon's Beck is a quarter of a mile above Yarm Bridge. Eaglescliffe stands on the opposite side to Yarm. Here there are inns. A mile and a quarter below Yarm Bridge the River Leven enters. A mile and a quarter still lower, opposite Barwick, Eaglescliffe Junction Station stands wide of the river.

Below on both sides to Stockton permission to fish can be had from the owners and tenants, and below Stockton to the sea the fishing is practically open. In the lower reaches the eel fishing is very good, eels being both large and numerous. Other coarse fish, roach and flounders principally. Three and a half miles below Barwick is Thornaby. Stockton Bridge is a mile and a half lower down. At Stockton there are numerous inns and two railway stations. Newport is two and three-quarter miles below Stockton Bridge. Middlesborough is two and a quarter miles lower down. Just below Newport Ferry the Thorpe Beck enters. This holds some capital fish, and is in the hands of the Stockton Club. All trout, except in the lower reaches, where there are pike, and perch (see above). The river reaches the sea seven miles below Middlesborough. The total length of the Tees is 102½ miles.

RIVER URE.

The River Ure rises at Ure Heads, on Lunds Fell, High Abbotside, 2,100 feet above sea level, in a wild moorland district. In flowing through Hell Beck Lunds, it gathers several small moorland streams, which drain from Abbotside on the east and Grisdale Common on the west. The principal tributaries are Cotterdale Beck, Widdale Beck, Hardraw Beck, and Gayle Beck, all of which join the river in the order named above Hawes. At Bainbridge the River Bain enters. This is an important angling stream, and runs from Lake Semmerwater. Then come the Bishopdale and Walden Becks, and below Middleham the River Cover, at Masham the River Burn, and at Ripon the River Skell, which receives the Laver. These are the most important tributaries (see *ante*). The Hawes and Northallerton Branch Railway runs parallel with the river from Hawes Junction to Leyburn.

The fishing on the Ure is very good, the grayling fishing being of the highest quality. On all the length of the river generally it is better grayling than trout water. The best lengths are perhaps, Ripon Club length and Sir Reginald Graham's and Lord Bolton's; the best grayling length being the Hawes Club water. The Wensleydale Club water can be fished without wading. Above Aysgarth the angler is not troubled with salmon smelts, as the salmon cannot get above Aysgarth Falls. The salmon fishing on the river is all in private hands. The river is a succession of streams and pools above Ripon. Below Bishop Monkton Cut the river is navigable, and from that place the deeps commence. These are confined to coarse fish. There is some good pike fishing at Boroughbridge.

From the source to Ure Foss (four miles) the fishing is no good. From Ure Foss to Yore Bridge, near Askrigg (about eleven and a quarter miles), the fishing on both sides, without any break of importance, belongs to the Hawes and High Abbotside Angling Association. President, Earl Wharncliffe; vice-president, J. C. C. Routh, Esq.; hon. secretary, Mr. Beckwith Thompson, Crown Hotel, Hawes. River watcher, James Blades. Sixty members. Not limited. Annual subscription for residents in the district, 5s.;

boys, and men coming under the heading of labourers, 2s. the season. All owners and occupiers supplied with free members' tickets. Non-residents' season tickets, 10s. Day tickets, 1s. No weekly or monthly tickets. From the commencement of the season to May 1st, angling is not permitted before 6 a.m. nor after 8 p m.; during May and September, before 4 a.m. nor after 10 p.m. During June, July, and August, angling is permitted on week days throughout the whole twenty-four hours. Trout season commences March 16th, and ends on October 1st; grayling season commences October 7th, ends February 1st. Members paying 5s. or upwards for trout tickets are not required to take out grayling tickets. Price of grayling tickets for non-members, 1s. each; and for non-residents, 1s. per day, or 5s. the season. No fish under 6in. allowed to be taken. All tickets procurable at the Crown Hotel, Hawes. No illegal baits allowed. All the tributary becks between Ure Foss and Hawes are also in the hands of the club, and afford good fishing. They are amenable to the above rules. The lower part of the club length is best for grayling. All the length is good for trout. About a quarter of a mile from Ure Foss is the Moor Cock Inn, which is one mile from Hawes Junction on the Settle and Carlisle Railway. Starting at Ure Foss, the places *en route* are Hardraw (five miles), inn; Appersett (five miles); Hawes (six miles), inns and railway station, fishing tickets at Crown Hotel; Buttersett (eight miles); and Yore Bridge (eleven and a quarter miles). At Yore Bridge, Bainbridge stands on the right bank and Askrigg on the left. Inns at both places, which are good centres for anglers. Also a railway station.

The Wensleydale Angling Association water commences at Yore Bridge, and extends on the left side of the river to Bear Park, about half-a-mile above Yore Mills Bridge, and on the right side to Yore Mills Bridge, Aysgarth, with one slight break at Cravenholme Farm, Bainbridge. President, F. Chapman, Esq.; hon. secretary and treasurer, W. Balderstone, Esq., Yore Bridge House, Bainbridge *viâ* Bedale. Number of members unlimited. Annual subscription, 10s. 6d.; any donor of £5 or upwards becomes a life member; boys under sixteen and men in condition of labourers supplied with tickets at 1s. 6d. each, residents only;

non-members' tickets, 2s. 6d. per day. Members can demand to see tickets. All trout under 7in. to be returned. Season commences March 16th, ends October 1st. No illegal baits allowed. Wading in the association waters strictly prohibited, except in Lake Semmerwater for the purpose of fishing the stone-fly. The association also have the fishing in Lake Semmerwater and the River Bain (see *ante*). There is a heavy stock of fish on this length of the Ure, but they are not such free risers as on the Wharfe or the Swale, although they run larger. Plenty of grayling up to 1lb. weight. No coarse fish except in Semmerwater, where there are quantities of rudd and bream. Crayfish are plentiful.

Bainbridge stands on the right bank at Yore Bridge. There is a good inn for anglers, this being the best centre both for fishing the Ure, the Bain, and Lake Semmerwater. Askrigg Railway Station is on the left bank, about a quarter of a mile below Yore Bridge. There are also good inns at Askrigg. It is five and a half miles from Yore Bridge to the commencement of Bear Park, on the left side, where the Wensleydale Angling Association ends. On the right side it is six miles from Yore Bridge to Aysgarth or Yore Mills Bridge, which is the bottom limit of the Wensleydale Angling Association length. From Aysgarth Bridge it is half-a-mile to Aysgarth, quarter of a mile to Palmer Flat, and three-quarters of a mile to Carperby, at all of which places there are inns. Aysgarth Railway Station is a quarter of a mile from Aysgarth Bridge.

From Aysgarth Bridge to the top side of Hackfall Woods, a distance of twenty-three miles following the course of the river, the whole of the fishing is private on both sides. The principal owners are Lord Bolton and Lord Masham. Permission to fish the water from Wensley Bridge to Ulshaw Bridge can sometimes be had on application to Lord Bolton's steward; or the landlords of the Bolton Arms and Golden Lion, Leyburn, can get permission for visitors staying at their hotels. Redmire Wath is two miles and a half below Aysgarth Bridge. Redmire, where there are inns and a railway station, is half-a-mile from the river. A mile below Redmire Wath, Lord Bolton's Park commences, half-a-mile below which, on the opposite side, is West Witton. Wensley is one mile and three-quarters below West Witton. At Wensley there is an inn. It is one mile to Wensley Station, and a mile and a half to Leyburn, where there are inns and a railway station. Two miles and a half below Wensley is Middleham Suspension Bridge, from which it is half-a-mile to Middleham (where there are several inns), and one and a quarter miles to Leyburn Railway Station. A mile and a half below Middleham Suspension Bridge is Spennithorne, where there is an inn and a railway station. A mile and a quarter below Spennithorne is Cover Bridge Inn. Mrs. Towler, of the Cover Bridge Inn ; Mr. Metcalfe, of the Red Lion ; and Mr. Rennie, Temperance Hotel, East Witton, can get permission for visitors staying at their houses to fish the south side of the Ure, from Ulshaw Bridge to Kilgram Bridge. Just below Ulshaw Bridge, the River Cover enters. This is an important angling tributary (see *ante*). Kilgram Bridge is four miles below Ulshaw Bridge, and three miles from Jervaulx Railway Station. Masham Bridge is five and a quarter miles below Kilgram Bridge. There are several inns and a railway station at Masham. One and a quarter miles below Masham Bridge the River Burn enters. This is an excellent trout stream, but strictly private. The top end of Hackfall Woods is two and three-quarter miles below Masham Bridge. This is the commencement of the Tanfield Club water. The Tanfield Angling Club water extends from the top side of Hackfall Woods to Bell Flask, a distance of six and a quarter miles. The limits on the left are from Black Robin Wood to Bell Flask without a break, and on the right side from the High side of Hackfall to the weir below Tanfield, with three breaks of private water—namely from the bottom of Hackfall Woods to Mickley Woods, from Mickley Mill to Low Mill Rush, and from opposite Slenningford Hall to Grensett Butts. The club is limited to thirty members. President, the Marquis of Ripon ; vice-president, Thomas Arton, Esq., of Tanfield Lodge ; treasurer, Mr. W. G. McLaughlin ; hon. sec., Mr. Francis M. Walbran, Northern Anglers' Depot, New Station Street, Leeds. Annual subscription, £4 4s. ; entrance fee, £3 3s. Three-day tickets during each season are granted each member at 2s. 6d. each for the use of a friend, who must accompany the member. Trout season, April 1st to October 1st ; grayling season, August 1st to February 15th. No trout to be taken under 8in. Lures permissible. Artificial fly, minnow, and worm. River watcher, Ralph Coldbeck. This club was only formed last season. They have erected a hatchery capable of accommodating 100,000 ova, and 30,000 have been hatched out this year. A rearing pond is in the course of erection, and in the last twelve months nearly 500 yearling fish, a great number seven inches in length, have been turned into the club's water.

From Black Robin Wood to Bell Flask is six miles. From the top side of Hackfall Woods to Tanfield Weir is four and a half miles. Tanfield is half-a-mile above the weir. This is the best centre for anglers. There is good accommodation at the inn, also a railway station. Mickley is two miles and a quarter above Tanfield, and Grewelthorpe stands above Hackfall. There are inns at both places. From the bottom limit of the Tanfield Club length at Bell Flask to Hutton Conyers, three and a quarter miles, the fishing is private on both sides. At the Mill Deep, at Hutton Conyers, the Ripon Angling Club's water commences, and extends on both sides of the river without a break to Hewick Bridge, with the exception of a very short length near the upper boundary. The best waters of the club are those on the Skell and Laver (see *ante*). President, Thomas Judson, Esq.; hon. secretary and treasurer, Mr. Arthur J. M. Wood, Bellwood, Ripon; river watcher, Thos. Marshall, Bondgate Green, Ripon. Limited to thirty members; always full. Annual subscription, £1 5s.; entrance fee, £1 10s. A member may take out a transferable ticket for £1 5s., or a day ticket for 5s., for the use of friends not residing less than five miles from Ripon; not more than two or three day tickets issued per week. Tickets for outsiders, 1s. 6d. per day, available for the Ure only; procurable from the hon. secretary, or Mr. Hodgson, gunsmith, Middle Street, Ripon; also at the Station Hotel, for the convenience of strangers coming in by train. Close time: trout, October 2nd to March 15th; grayling, March 15th to June 15th. Nothing but artificial fly allowed for trout until May 1st. All trout under 7in. to be returned. All rods used on the waters to be marked with that length. No dogs allowed. The whole of the fishing is good, the private lengths on the Skell and the Laver being first-class. On these lengths there is nothing but trout, except the lowest half of the Skell. Coarse fish abound in the Ure.

From Mill Deep to Hewick Bridge is about three miles. Ripon Bridge is about mid-distance. Here there are inns and a railway station. The River Skell enters about half-a-mile above Hewick Bridge. From Hewick Bridge to Bishop Monkton Cut (one and three-quarter miles), on the right side, permission to fish may be had from the steward, Mr. F. J. Sharp, Newby Estate Office, Ripon. Only a limited number of tickets are issued.

From Hewick Bridge on the left side, to Boroughbridge, the fishing is private; but below Newby Park permission may be had occasionally from the riparian owners. From Bishop Monkton Cut to Westwick Lock (one and a half miles) the fishing is strictly private. Bishop Monkton, where there are inns, is one mile from the river. The nearest railway station is Wormald Green, three miles.

From Westwick Lock to Roecliffe, on the right side, the steward, Mr. F. J. Sharp, Newby Estate Office, Ripon, grants a limited number of tickets yearly. Roecliffe is one and a half miles below Westwick Lock. From Roecliffe (inn) on the right side, to below Aldborough Park, permission to fish may occasionally be obtained from A. S. Lawson, Esq., Aldborough Manor.

Langthorpe, where there is an inn, is a mile and a quarter below Roecliffe. Permission to fish at Langthorpe, on the left side, must be obtained from Mr. Gates and other owners. Boroughbridge is half-a-mile below Langthorpe. The fishing about the bridge is open. Here there is a railway station and several inns.

The Station Hotel is an angler's resort. Landlord, Mr. W. A. Lister, is pleased to afford anglers any information. The Harrogate Angling Association have a standing permit to fish the water on the north side from the bridge to 200 yards below Milby Lock (about three-quarters of a mile). Below this to the River Swale and on the other side opposite Aldborough Park the Harrogate Conservative Angling Club have fishing rights. See Oak Beck.

Ellingthorpe Ings are two miles below Boroughbridge, on the left side. Aldborough Park boundary is three-quarters of a mile below Boroughbridge, on the right side. From this boundary to the mouth of the river, permission to fish must be had from Major

Staypleton, Myton Hall, and others. The river Ure joins the Swale in forming the source of the Ouse at Swale Nab, two miles and three-quarters below Boroughbridge. The total length of the river is sixty-six and three-quarter miles. The Board of Conservators have recently turned a thousand yearling trout into the Ure about Ripon.

"**THE URE**" (No. 3 of the Yorkshire Rivers Series), with bird's-eye view of the roads and surrounding country, by Tom Bradley, being a most complete angler's or tourist's guide, showing all places of note on the banks of the river, with brief descriptions of the legends and folk lore of the district. May be obtained at the office of *The Yorkshire Post*, Leeds, or ordered through any bookseller, price 6d., by post 7½d.

RIVER WENNING.

The River Wenning commences about a mile south of Clapham, at the confluence of the Clapham and Austwick Becks, which rise from the Clapham and Austwick Moors respectively, the former having its source in Clapham Bottom, and draining the limestone hills adjoining, the latter running from Crummack Dale below Moughton Scars and draining Moughton side. These two streams are the principal tributaries of the Wenning, and both hold fish in the bottom reaches. Tickets to fish the same are procurable at the Flying Horse Shoe Inn, Clapham. The only other tributary of importance is Keasden Beck. After leaving the limestone hills, the streams that fall to the river in its course drain the hills that lie under the south-east slopes of Ingleborough, and those that fall from the north side of Bowland Forest. The fishing is very good on the whole length of the river, although the fish run somewhat small. Nothing but trout above Lower Bentham Mill Weir. The salmon and sprods and morts do not get above that point, but below, the fishing for them is very good in September and October.

From the confluence of Clapham and Austwick Becks to Mere Gill Beck (three and a quarter miles), tickets to fish on the right or

Clapham side of the river can be had from Mr. Henry Coates, Flying Horse Shoe Inn, Clapham. The six-monthly season tickets expire on October 1st. Tom Clark is the river watcher. Any kind of legal bait allowed. On the opposite side to this water and down to Lower Bentham Bridge on both sides, permission may be had from the tenants. There is little difficulty in gaining permission so long as anglers conduct themselves properly. Wenning Bridge is three-quarters of a mile below the source, and Clapham Station is one mile from the bridge. Skew Bridge is two miles below the source, and Keasden Beck enters half-a-mile below this bridge. Bloe Beck enters a little below Keasden Beck. Greystone Gill Bridge is three-quarters of a mile below Mere Gill Beck, and Mill Beck enters a quarter of a mile below that bridge. Bentham Bridge is almost two miles below Greystone Gill Bridge. There are inns and a railway station at Bentham. Lower Bentham Bridge is a mile and a half below Bentham Bridge. Below Lower Bentham Bridge the fishing is strictly private on both sides until it crosses the county boundary. At Lower Bentham there is a weir and an inn. Church Bridge is a quarter of a mile lower down. Eskew Beck enters just below Church Bridge. Here the river crosses the county boundary on the left, and a mile and a half below Lower Bentham it leaves the county of York entirely. From the source to the county boundary the length of the stream is eight and three-quarter miles. The Wenning enters the River Lune about one mile below Hornby Castle. The total length of the river is thirteen miles.

RIVER WENT.

The River Went commences a little above Ackworth Carr Bridge, about three miles south of Pontefract, where the Went Beck is joined by another small stream. It runs through a somewhat undulating country past Wentbridge, Stapleton Park, and Kirk Smeaton to Norton, whence it traverses a dead level country to the River Don, which it enters about a mile above the commencement of the Dutch River (see *ante*). This latter portion of the river is known as the Went Drainage. The river is navigable as far as

Kirk Smeaton, and would be tidal but for the fact of there being a lock at Went Mouth, so that the tides which flow up the Don considerably beyond this point do not affect it. The best of the fishing is in the hands of the Went Drainage, perch, eels and pike being fairly good. The top part of the stream to Old Bridge below Smeaton Crags is private. Below Old Bridge to Norton Weir, permission can be had from owners and tenants, and below Norton Mill Dam to Went End, application must be made to Mr. E. E. Clark, clerk to the Went Drainage, or to George Goodridge, the lock-keeper, Went End, Cowick *via* Selby.

Wentbridge is three and a quarter miles below the source. Here the Great North Road, Doncaster to Ferrybridge, crosses the river. Kirk Smeaton on the Hull and Barnsley railway is the nearest station. At Wentbridge there is an inn. Brokendale's Bridge is a mile and a quarter below Wentbridge and Smeaton Crags, and the Old Bridge about a quarter of a mile lower down. A mile below Old Bridge is Hodge Bridge, Kirk Smeaton. Little Smeaton is on the opposite side of the river. Here there is a railway station and inns at both places. Willow Bridge is three-quarters of a mile below. From this bridge it is two miles to Womersley station. Three-quarters of a mile below Willow Bridge is Norton Mill Weir and Bridge. The Priory Bridge is a quarter of a mile lower down. Norton stands half-a-mile wide of the river. The Lancashire and Yorkshire Railway Bridge crosses half-a-mile below Priory Bridge, and just above this railway bridge is Tan Pit Bridge. Boister's Bridge is a mile below Priory Bridge, and Doncaster and Selby Road Bridge crosses half-a-mile below. Fenwick Bridge is three miles below the road bridge, and Topham Ferry Bridge is two miles below Fenwick. From Topham Ferry Bridge it is half-a-mile to Sykehouse. Here there are inns. A mile below the Ferry Bridge is the Balm Croft Bridge, and Went Mouth is two and a half miles lower down. About a quarter of a mile above Went Mouth a bridge crosses. At Went Mouth there is a lock, and here the lock-keeper, George Goodricke, lives. The river enters the Don opposite Bank Side House. Snaith is the nearest station, three miles. The total length of the river is eighteen miles.

RIVER WISKE.

The River Wiske and Codbeck are the two principal tributaries of the Lower Swale. The Wiske commences at Staddle Bridge, 237 feet above sea level on the Thirsk and Stockton highway, near to Tontine Inn and Mount Grace Priory, and about one and a half miles west of the source of Codbeck. The infant stream is a continuation of Carr Beck, which rises at the foot of the Cleveland Hills. The stream is very irregular in its course, which is crowded with small turnings, and running the whole of its course through an almost dead level country. From Staddle Bridge it runs north to West Routon, and thence due west to Great Smeaton, within a short distance of the Tees, from which place it turns due south, past Danby Wiske, Northallerton, and Otterington to the Swale, making almost a circle in its course. The stream is fishable from source to mouth. It is a dead, slow-running stream. There is nothing but coarse fishing, which, however, is very good. Pike, perch, chub, and eels. Northallerton, where there is good accommodation, is the best centre. By the highway Staddle Bridge is eleven miles from Thirsk and nine miles from Yarm.

From Staddle Bridge to North Otterington Bridge, a distance of twenty-three and a half miles, following the winding of the stream, permission to fish may be had from the owners and tenants, which, in most cases, is readily granted. Bank Bridge is a mile and a quarter below Staddle Bridge. It is a mile to East Harsley, and three-quarters of a mile to Ingleby Arncliffe. Inns at both places, also two miles to Welbury Station. A mile and three-quarters below Bank Bridge, East Routon Stell enters. East Routon Bridge is a mile and a half lower down. West Routon Bridge is three-quarters of a mile below. Inns at both places. It is one and three-quarter miles from the bridge to Welbury Station. Three-quarters of a mile below West Routon Bridge the Leeds and Northern Railway crosses. Appleton Wiske Bridge is a mile and a quarter below the railway bridge. Inns at Appleton Wiske. Smeaton Bridge is three miles below Appleton Wiske. From Smeaton Bridge it is nine and a half miles to Darlington, and six and a half to Northallerton. There are inns at Great Smeaton, and East Cowton is the nearest station, two miles. Three miles below Smeaton Bridge is Birkby Bridge. From this bridge it is one and a half miles to East Cowton, where there are inns and a railway station. A quarter of a mile below Birkby the York and Newcastle Railway Bridge crosses. Two miles and a half below the railway bridge is Danby Wiske Bridge. There are inns at Danby Wiske. Three miles and a half below Danby Wiske is Yafforth Bridge. There is an inn at Yafforth, and it is one and a half miles to Northallerton Station.

A mile below Yafforth, Bedale Branch Railway Bridge crosses. Willow Beck enters three-quarters of a mile lower down, and Howden Bridge is just below. From this bridge it is one mile to Ainderby Steeple, where there are inns and a railway station, one mile to Romanby, and one and a quarter miles to Northallerton Station. Two miles and a quarter below Howden Bridge is North Otterington Bridge.

From North Otterington Bridge to South Otterington Bridge the fishing is private. Three-quarters of a mile below North Otterington Bridge is the Leeds and Northern Railway Bridge and Newby Wiske Station. Newby Wiske, where there is an inn, is half-a-mile below, and South Otterington Bridge one mile. There are inns at South Otterington.

From South Otterington Bridge to a little above Kirkby Bridge the fishing is private, but permission may occasionally be had from the owners or tenants. Kirkby Bridge is two and a quarter miles below South Otterington. Kirkby Wiske, where there is an inn, stands on the right bank.

From Kirkby Wiske to Wiske Mouth the river is private on both sides. Privet Bridge is about a quarter of a mile below Kirby Bridge, and Wiske Mouth is two miles below. Here the Wiske enters the Swale opposite Pickhill. The total length of the river is twenty-nine and a half miles.

RIVER WHARFE.

The Wharfe springs at Outershaw Moss, on Cam Fell, 1,440 feet above the sea. Above the hamlet of Outershaw it is called Outershaw Beck. Numerous small streams from Outershaw Side and Outershaw Moss run into this beck. The principal tributaries of the river are the River Skirfare, the River Washburn, and the River Cock (see *ante*), besides numerous considerable becks from source to mouth. Above Ilkley the river is a succession of streams and pools. Below that place the deeps commence, although there are occasional streams. The river is tidal below Tadcaster Weir, from which point downwards it is a deep, sluggish stream, with sedgy banks.

The fishing in the Wharfe is excellent throughout, the trout and grayling in the higher reaches being of the highest quality. Below Tadcaster the river is confined to coarse fish of all kinds except salmon, which fishing is in private hands. Flounders are also abundant in the lower reaches. Above Tadcaster both trout and grayling begin to put in an appearance. In the middle reaches, the Otley Club length is the best. At Burley the fishing begins to improve, and from Ilkley upwards the improvement gradually increases to the top limit of the Kilnsey Club, whose length of water is the best on the river. The Upper Wharfe is confined to trout and grayling. The latter however, are not found above Netherside Falls. From Bolton Abbey the railway runs along the valley parallel with the river to Arthington.

From the source to Buckden the fishing is in the hands of the tenants, from whom permission may be obtained. The fish run very small, however, except for a few miles above Buckden.

Buckden is the highest centre for the top end of the dale; good inns. Nearest railway station, Skipton. Mail cart carries passengers from Skipton to all the villages between that place and Buckden. From Buckden to Starbottom (two miles) the fishing is private.

At Starbottom the Kilnsey Angling Club length commences, and extends on both sides of the river to Netherside without a break, with the exception of two or three small fields. This club has also two miles of water on the Skirfare (see *post*). The club committee consists of six members. Hon. secretary and treasurer, Captain Henderson. River watchers, Jerry Emmott (Kilnsey) and David Mallinson (Kettlewell). Number of members limited to thirty-five. Annual subscription, £4 14s. 6d.; entrance fee, £2

12s. 6d. A few day tickets at five shillings each are issued to visitors staying at Kilnsey and the inns north of that place, procurable from the keepers. Trout fishing very good. Close time, October 1st to March 16th. Limit of trout, 7in. Part of the river open to all kinds of legitimate lures, part closed to everything but artificial fly until after June 20th. From the top to the bottom limit of the club, following the course of the river, it is seven and a half miles. The villages *en route* are Kettlewell, Kilnsey, and Coniston.

At Netherside, the Kilnsey Club length ends, and the Linton, Threshfield, and Grassington Anglers' Club commences. Their water extends to about a mile below Linton Church, where it joins the Burnsall Club. There are a few short breaks on both sides of the river--namely, the private water of the Rev. T. W. Nowell, at Netherside, about a quarter of a mile, and a short piece of about one field belonging to the Linton Falls Creamery. On the Grassington side of the river there is a short piece of fishing opposite Linton Mill, which belongs to Mrs. Hartley. On this, the left side, the Grassington Club water ends at Linton Stepping Stones. President of the Grassington Club, the Rev. T. W. Nowell; vice-presidents, Messrs. William Field and George Owram; secretary and treasurer, Mr. William Harker, Grassington, near Skipton; committee, Messrs. George Hardacre, Joseph Baxendale, and Thomas Twing; river watcher, James Town, Mill, Linton, Skipton. Number of members, thirty, not limited. Annual subscription, 10s. Day tickets, 2s. 6d., procurable from the secretary, or Mr. G. Owram, Linton, and Mr. Robert Metcalf, Threshfield. Season commences March 16th, ends October 1st; grayling season ends March 15th. No nets, night lines, or medicated baits allowed. Fishing good, both trout and grayling. From Netherside to Linton Church it is two miles. The villages *en route* are Threshfield, Linton, and Grassington, which all have inns. From Linton it is eight miles to Skipton Station and nine miles to Bolton Abbey Station.

At Linton Stepping Stones the Grassington Club length ends on the left side, and the Appletreewick, Barden, and Burnsall Angling Club commences. The top limit is Linton Stepping Stones, the bottom limit Barden Bridge. On the north side—that is, the Hebden and Appletreewick side—there is a break—viz., the water belonging to the New Inn, Appletreewick, which can only be fished from that side by members who stay at the inn or take a meal there. The New Inn water is about a mile in length, free to visitors staying at the house. Day tickets for outsiders, 2s. 6d. each. On the south—or Burnsall—side, the whole length from the bottom limit of the Grassington Club to Barden Bridge belongs to Burnsall Club. This club is limited to fifty members. Annual subscription, £2 2s.; each member, besides his annual ticket, to have four day tickets for the use of friends, who shall only use the tickets in his company. Day tickets are issued to the general public at 5s. each, from April 1st to September 30th. Close time for trout, October 1st to March 31st; close time for grayling, February 1st to March 31st. All trout under 7in. and all spawning grayling to be returned to the river. None but members allowed to fish may-fly or creeper; below Drebley Stepping Stones artificial fly only. No bottom fishing allowed on the Duke of Devonshire's estates. No salmon spawn or medicated baits allowed on any part of the club length. Day tickets are procurable from Sylvester Lister, Barden Tower; Mr. Ramsden, New Inn, Appletreewick; J. W. Binns, Red Lion Inn, Burnsall; and the secretary, Mr. Thomas J. Critchley, Brook Street, Ilkley. Watcher's address, J. H. Martindale, Burnsall, *via* Skipton. Dogs prohibited. The committee, by request, give the following list of houses open to accommodate members or visitors: J. A. Bland, Woodhouse, near Burnsall; Mr. Brown, Lythe House, Hebden; Mr. Ramsden, New Inn, Appletreewick; S. Lister, Barden Tower; J. W. Binns, Red Lion Inn, Burnsall; and J. H. Martindale, Burnsall.

At Barden Bridge, the Appletreewick, Barden, and Burnsall Club water ends, and the Bolton Woods length commences. From Barden Bridge to Bolton Bridge, both sides without a break, the fishing can be had free by staying at the Devonshire Arms or the Red Lion, Bolton Bridge—a day for each night up to eight days. Good trout and grayling. Close time for trout, October 2nd to March 31st. Nothing but fly permitted from April 1st to October 1st. No bottom-fishing allowed. All trout under 8in. to be returned. No Sunday fishing. Watcher has power to examine tickets and panniers. Watcher, Sylvester Lister, Barden Tower; keeper, Thos. Holmes, Stouths, Bolton Abbey. From Barden Bridge to Bolton Bridge, following the course of the river, it is four and a-quarter miles. Barden Tower adjoins Barden Bridge. Here the Duke of Devonshire's watcher, Sylvester Lister, lives. Refreshments, and tickets for fishing the Burnsall Club length can be obtained. Railway stations—Bolton Abbey, four and a-quarter miles; Skipton, six and a-quarter miles. The nearest stations to Bolton Bridge are Bolton Abbey, three-quarters of a mile; Addingham, two and a-half miles; Skipton, six miles.

The Bolton Woods length ends at Morley Beck, immediately below Bolton Bridge, and the private water of Farfield Hall commences. The fishing on both sides is in private hands to Addingham Low Weir, the only break being the Leeds and County Club length, which commences on the right, or Addingham side, at Farfield Park boundary, one and a-half miles below Bolton Bridge, and extends (about half-a-mile) to the top end of Addingham Hall Mill Weir. The Leeds and County Angling Association is the oldest legitimate angling club in Leeds. Patrons: Right Hon. W. L. Jackson, M.P.; Capt. P. P. Galwey; John Barran, Esq., M.P.; Herbert Gladstone, Esq., M.P. President, Mr. W. H. Bradford; vice-president, Mr. C. Hogg; hon. sec., Mr. Geo. Helliwell, 130, Hyde Park Road, Leeds. Thirty members. Annual subscription, £1; entrance fee, £2. The club length on the Wharfe is good water, and holds a nice lot of trout. In addition to this water, they have Roundhay Beck to Killingbeck Pond, near Leeds, the two ponds at Killingbeck, and the beck which runs from them to the river Aire, near Swillington. There are some good fish in this beck and the ponds. Addingham, where there are several inns and a railway station, lies on the right of the river, about half-a-mile from the bottom limit of the club length. Skipton is six and three-quarter miles distant.

Addingham Low Weir is a mile below the Leeds and County Club length. Here the Ilkley Angling Club water begins, and extends on the Ilkley side to Ben Rhydding Bridge, and on the Denton side to Bow Beck. President, C. M. Middleton, Esq.; vice-presidents, T. H. Bracken, Esq., Major Middleton, J.P.;

Edward Middleton, Esq., D'arcy Wyvill, Esq., E. H. Wade, Esq., and Henry Ellis, Esq.; hon. sec., J. Green, Esq., Ilkley; river watcher, Thomas Senior, Ash Grove, Ilkley. Limited to forty-five members. Annual subscription, £2 12s. 6d.; entrance fee, £1 11s. 6d. Day tickets are issued to residents or *bona-fide* visitors sleeping in Ilkley or Ben Rhydding at 5s. per day, and may be obtained from Mr. T. G. Critchley, Brook Street, Ilkley. Anglers to keep to the river-side. Dogs prohibited. Close time: trout, October 2nd to March 15th; grayling, February 15th to June 15th. All trout and grayling under 8in. to be returned. No medicated bait or bottom fishing allowed. The fishing is very good; plenty of trout and grayling, and a few coarse fish. The length of the club water from Addingham Low Weir to Bow Beck on the Denton side is three and a-half miles, and to Ben Rhydding Bridge, on the Ilkley side, four and a-half miles. Ilkley, where there are numerous hotels and a railway station, is two miles below the top limit. At Bow Beck, on the Denton side, the private water of John Wormald, Esq., of Denton Hall, commences, and below the Ilkley Club length the fishing is private on both sides to Otley Bridge, which is five miles below Ben Rhydding Bridge. *En route* is Burley, on the right side of the river, where there are several inns and a railway station. At Burley, the fishing, which is strictly private, belongs to F. W. Fison, Esq., of Greenholme. On the opposite side it belongs to Colonel Dawson, of Weston Hall. At Otley there are numerous inns and a railway station.

At Otley Bridge the Otley Angling Club commences, and extends on the Farnley or left side to Harewood Bridge, and on the Otley side to below Pool Bridge with the exception of Mr. Garnett's portion of the river and two fields at Pool. President, Ayscough Fawkes, Esq., Farnley Hall; vice-president, Francis Darwin, Esq., Creskeld; hon. secretary, Mr. R. M. Pratt, Manor Square, Otley; river watcher, H. Spreckley, Pool. Limited to thirty members. Annual subscription, £3; entrance fee, £2. No short period tickets issued. Close time: trout, October 2nd to April 1st; grayling, February 15th to June 15th. No bobbing or natural fly fishing allowed. No Sunday fishing. Fish under 7in. to be returned. Lures permissible: artificial worm and minnow.

Besides trout and grayling, there are chub, dace, barbel, gudgeon, eels, and minnows. The club have a hatchery and rearing ponds and turn fry and yearling fish out annually. Last year over 3,000 were placed in the river. Two miles below Otley Bridge the River Washburn, a first-class trout stream (see *ante*), enters on the left side. On the right side, three and a half miles below Otley Bridge, is Pool, where there are inns and a railway station. Here are two fields, one on either side of the bridge, in which fishing may be obtained by applying to the landlord of the White Hart, Pool. Below Pool Corn Mill there is one field belonging to the Otley Club, below which the Holbeck Angling Society's private water commences. The bottom limit being opposite Riffa Beck end. The club water lies on the right or Pool side of the river, adjoining three fields. About half-a-mile below the first field, Mr. Swallow's house and grounds come in, where the fishing is private ; then come the other two fields belonging to the club. President, Mr. James Dull ; vice-president, Mr. F. Coates ; hon. secretary, Mr. W. Ingham, 8, Staincross Street, Holbeck, Leeds ; river watcher, Mr. Spreckley, Pool. Limited to seventy members. Annual subscription, 12s. 6d. ; entrance fee, 5s. ; Amalgamation fee, 1s. 4d. No tickets for outsiders. Dates of close time and restrictions same as Yorkshire Fishery Board. Some good trout fishing, also dace, chub, and eels. A mile and a half below Pool Bridge, Arthington Viaduct (Leeds and Harrogate Railway) crosses the river. At Arthington there is an inn and railway station, half-a-mile distant.

From the bottom limit of Holbeck Club length on the right side, and Otley Club on the left, the water below to Collingham Bridge is private on both sides. Permission to fish a portion of it may occasionally be obtained on application to the Earl of Harewood's steward, Mr. Moorson, at the Harewood Estate Offices. Harewood Bridge, following the course cf the river, is four and a half miles below Arthington Viaduct ; Woodhall Bridge, eight miles ; and Collingham Bridge, ten and a quarter miles. From Harewood Bridge to Harewood village (right side), where there is an inn, is one mile, and to Leeds eight and a half miles. From Woodhall Bridge to East Keswick (right side), one mile ; inn and railway station. At Woodhall (left side) the fishing is strictly private, but below Woodhall Park on that side to Flint Mill, which is below Wetherby, permission to fish may occasionally be had from the tenants. On the right, or Collingham side, Lord Harewood's water ends about three-quarters of a mile below Woodhall Bridge, a little above Langwith Wood, where the private water or Colonel Gunter commences, and runs without a break to Flint Mill Weir. Permission may sometimes be had to fish the lengths above Wetherby Bridge. At Collingham there are inns and a railway station (Leeds and Wetherby Branch). On the opposite side of the river is Linton village. Here the Collingham Beck enters the river. It is a good trout stream. Permission to fish the bottom end (about three-quarters of a mile) may be had from the tenants. The top end is the private fishing of George Lane Fox, Esq.

From Collingham Bridge to Wetherby Bridge is two and a quarter miles. Wetherby stands on the left bank. There are numerous inns and a railway station. Above the bridge is a weir, where there is a salmon ladder. Below the bridge, on the right side, Colonel Gunter's park commences, and the fishing is strictly private to Flint Mill Weir, one and three-quarter miles below. On the Wetherby side permission is required from the tenants. Below Flint Mill to St. Helen's Well on the left bank, and to Fir Green Beck on the right—also the length from St. Helen's Ford to Newton Kyme on the right bank—the river is fishable by written permits, to be obtained free of cost from Mr. Andrew Halliday, Royal Hotel, Boston Spa. As these permits are granted on sufferance, anglers are cautioned against doing damage to crops or property. St. Helen's Ford is three miles below Flint Mill; Fir Green Beck, two and a quarter miles; and Thorp Arch Bridge one and a half miles. Thorp Arch is on the left bank. Boston Spa is on the opposite bank. Fishing permits obtained at the Royal Hotel. Thorp Arch Railway Station, one mile; Collingham Station, two and three-quarter miles.

Fir Green Beck is a private trout stream belonging to George Lane Fox, Esq. It runs from Bramham Park, through Bramham village, to the river, and has recently been well-stocked with trout. Below Fir Green Beck to St. Helen's Ford the fishing is private.

From St. Helen's Ford to Newton Kyme permits granted as above. Below St. Helen's Ford on the left side there is a short length, about half-a-mile, fishable by permission from the tenants. Thence to Tadcaster Weir it is strictly private. Newton Kyme is three-quarters of a mile below St. Helen's Ford, on the right bank. Here there is a railway station. Permission to fish from here to the low boundary of Newton Kyme Park can be had from Messrs. John Smith and Son, Tadcaster Brewery, about one and three-quarter miles. Below to Tadcaster Weir, the fishing is private. Tadcaster Weir is three and a quarter miles below Newton Kyme.

The Tadcaster Angling and Preservation Society's water commences at Tadcaster Weir. President, Wm. Smith, Esq.; hon. secretary and treasurer, Mr. W. Holloway, Bridge End, Tadcaster. Water bailiff, W. Welsh. About sixty members. No one admitted residing outside a seven-mile radius of Tadcaster. Annual subscription, 5s.; entrance fee, 1s.; respectable boys under sixteen years, 1s. per year. Daily tickets for outsiders, 6d.; weekly tickets, 2s. Outside clubs charged 2s. 6d. for every twenty members fishing a match. Tickets obtainable from the secretary, and from W. Dyson, at the Club House, Britannia Inn, Tadcaster. Close-time and restrictions same as Yorkshire Fishery Board. The club water extends on the left side from the Weir to the end of Owston Farm, without a break with the exception of one field called Shepherd's Garth, and on the right side the greater part between the dam and the bridge, and from Tadcaster Bridge to Cock Beck without a break. Chiefly coarse fish are there found. A few grayling and an occasional trout between the Mill Dam and the bridge. Prior to last season the fishing at Tadcaster has been mostly open, but the club have recently acquired most of the water; it is their intention to re-stock and improve their part of the river. The spring tides flow to Tadcaster Weir, and below the river is navigable. The length of the Tadcaster Club water is two and three-quarter miles on the left side, and one mile on the right. Tadcaster is on a branch of the Great North-road, and nine miles from York. There is a railway station and several inns. The salmon fishery belongs to John Fielden, Esq., of Grimstone Park, and fishing generally on this side from Cock Beck to Ulleskelf

Bridge is strictly private. Very few salmon. They rarely get above Grimstone Park.

From the end of Tadcaster Club water to Ulleskelf Railway Bridge (three-quarters of a mile), the fishing is strictly private on both sides. From the railway bridge to the confluence of the Wharfe with the Ouse, the fishing on the left, or Nun Appleton, side is owned by Sir Fred Milner, Bart., and is practically open except where Nun Appleton Park joins the river, which is strictly private. Anglers are allowed on sufferance to fish Sir Fred Milner's water so long as they conduct themselves like *bona-fide* sportsmen. On the right, or Ulleskelf, side the fishing is open from the railway bridge to the low side of Ulleskelf. Then comes a short length which belongs to Mr. Baynes, and another to Mr. Hodgson, which ends below Ossendike House, both of which are private, and from which point to the mouth of the river it is practically open fishing, tenants not interfering with anglers who conduct themselves properly.

Ulleskelf stands on the right bank of the river, half-a-mile below the railway bridge. Here there are inns and a railway station on the York and Leeds line. There is a ferry at Ulleskelf and a footpath on the left side of the river to Bolton Percy (three-quarters of a mile), where there is an inn and a railway station. The ordinary tides flow to Ulleskelf Ferry. From just below Ulleskelf to below Ossendike House, the private water is about a mile in length. Ryther is two and a half miles below Ulleskelf, the latter being the nearest railway station. At Ryther, which stands on the right bank, there are two inns. Nun Appleton Park is on the opposite bank. The neap tides flow to Ryther Hill Farm. From Ryther to Wharfe Mouth is two and three-quarter miles. There is a ferry at Nun Appleton and also at Wharfe Mouth, which is half-a-mile from Cawood, where there are several inns. The Wharfe joins the Ouse at Acaster Roving, the total length of the river, from source to mouth, measured down the centre of the stream, being seventy-nine and three-quarter miles.

"THE WHARFE" (No. 1 of the Yorkshire Rivers Series), with bird's-eye view of the roads and surrounding country, by Tom Bradley, being a most complete angler's or tourist's guide, showing all places of note on the banks of the river, with brief descriptions of the legends and folk lore of the district. May be obtained at the office of *The Yorkshire Post*, Leeds, or ordered through any bookseller, price 6d., by post 7½d.

RIVER WASHBURN.

The River Washburn is the most important tributary of the Wharfe. It rises 1,230 feet above the sea at Washburn Head, Greenhow Hill, on the south side of Craven Moor, and about half-a-mile south of the Skipton and Pateley Bridge highway. For the first few miles of its course it runs through a wild moorland district. When it reaches West End, above Blubberhouses, it enters one of the most charming valleys in Yorkshire, whose beauties increase until the river joins the Wharfe. The Leeds Corporation have utilised the natural formation of this valley for the construction of three large reservoirs, but they have preserved the fishing rights. The Washburn enters the first of these reservoirs (Fewston) at Blubberhouses Bridge. The embankment of the Fewston Reservoir forms the top end of the second reservoir (Swinsty). The old course of the river runs down the centre of the reservoirs, the overflow re-entering the river at the foot of Swinsty embankment, running thence for a couple of miles to the third, or Lindley Reservoir, from the bottom of which it runs through Lindley Woods by Leathley and Farnley to the Wharfe.

The fishing throughout is excellent, the top and bottom reaches being the best lengths; that from West End to Blubberhouses Bridge being probably the best on the river. Principally trout, which run about three to the pound. There are also a few grayling in the lengths from Lindley Reservoir to the Wharfe, and between Lindley and Swinsty Reservoirs, the latter length being the best, the grayling running about a pound and upwards. This length also contains some good eels. Gudgeon are somewhat too plentiful in the reservoirs. The top reservoir also holds some golden tench, which were introduced by Lord Walsingham.

The fishing is little or no good above Hodspith, which is three and a half miles from Washburn Head. Below to West End it is practically open, tenants allowing anglers to fish so long as they do no damage. This length of water extends for about a mile and a half. At West End, where there is an inn, the Capelshaw Beck enters. The bottom end of this beck holds some nice fish, the fishing being open. From West End to Blubberhouses (two and a half miles) the fishing is private on both sides, but permission may occasionally be had from owners to fish some portions of the stream, or on application to Mr. David Ingillby, landlord of the Frankland Arms, Blubberhouses, who can get permission for anglers. There is good accommodation for anglers at the Frankland Arms (see page 159).

Blubberhouses is the best centre for the fishing in the Washburn and reservoirs. Darley, on the Pateley Bridge branch, is the nearest railway station, being four miles distant. It is six and three-quarter miles to Bolton Bridge Station, and twelve miles to Skipton.

Lord Walsingham's private fishing commences a little above Blubberhouses Bridge, and extends down the right side of the river and Fewston Reservoir to Thackray Beck. Thackray Beck is one mile below Blubberhouses Bridge.

The water belonging to the Leeds Corporation begins at West House Mills, a short distance above Blubberhouses Bridge, and extends down the left side round Fewston Reservoir to Thackray Beck, where it joins Lord Walsingham's water. Anglers holding fishing orders are cautioned against trespassing on Lord Walsingham's part of the reservoir. The Corporation fishing also embraces the whole of Swinsty Reservoir. Fishing orders to fish any part of the Corporation water can be had on application to any member of the Leeds Corporation Waterworks Committee (chairman, Alderman Alf Cooke, Esq., J.P.) Each order allows the holder three days' fishing, and must be presented on each day to the reservoir keeper at Fewston (Mr. Storey) or Swinsty (Mr. Harris), that he may endorse the date thereon. The orders are not transferable. No Sunday fishing. No dogs allowed. No fishing between the hours of 9-0 p.m. and 7-0 a.m. Close time, October 1st to April 30th. No wading in either streams or reservoirs. No ground baiting or medicated baits allowed. One rod only.

Anglers are cautioned against doing any damage to the property of the Corporation. Fewston Reservoir starts at Blubberhouses Bridge, and extends to Fewston (two miles measured down the old river course) where the Swinsty Reservoir starts, and extends to below Swinsty Hall (one and a half miles). At Fewston there is an inn. There is a road across the Fewston Reservoir embankment which leads to Timble (inn) one mile, and Otley seven and a half miles ; also to Harrogate, eight miles.

From the bottom of Swinsty Reservoir embankment to the river Wharfe the whole of the fishing is private. From a little below Dob Park Bridge it belongs to Ayscough Fawkes, Esq., of Farnley Hall, who also holds the fishing rights in Lindley Reservoir and the whole of the stream from that place to the Wharfe. This reservoir is used by a firm of Leeds engineers for testing their torpedoes, and the fishing in it has fallen off a great deal, but the river below from the reservoir to the Wharfe is full of fish, and affords excellent sport.

The private water between the Swinsty and Lindley Reservoirs is two and a half miles long, the latter reservoir being a mile and a half in length. Dob Park Bridge is half-way between the two reservoirs, and three and a half miles from Otley, where there are several inns and a railway station. Mr. Fawkes's private water from Lindley Reservoir to the Wharfe is two and a quarter miles long. The Washburn enters the Wharfe at Washburn Foot, just below the village of Leathley. Leathley Bridge is one and a quarter miles from Pool, where there are inns and a railway station. The total length of the Washburn, measured down the old river course, is seventeen and a half miles.

REVISIONS AND CORRECTIONS.

1894.

Page 3.—The few fields mentioned near Kildwick Bridge, namely, the second and fourth fields and the Willow Garth, all above the bridge, the fishing is now in the hands of the Saltaire Angling Association (see page 5).

Page 10.—The Burniston Angling Club season is extended to September 30th.

Page 14.—The Thirsk Angling Club have re-stocked Codbeck with trout since the stream was poisoned last season, when hundreds of trout suffered in the two miles of water south of Thirsk, and stones of dead fish were got out between Thirsk and Sowerby. In some cases trout scaled 3lbs. and trout over 2lbs. All well fed and in beautiful colour.

Page 14, *line* 9.—Town End Bridge should read World End Bridge.

Page 15.—Huddersfield Angling Association have abandoned Woodside Reservoir. There are now no fish in it, and the Longwood Bottom Reservoir only holds trout yearlings at present. The membership of this club is now limited to fifty, and the privilege of taking a friend is withdrawn from honorary members.

Page 15.—Mr. Edward Mitchell, Scarborough, is now hon. sec. Costa Angling Club, *vice* Mr. J. H. Philips, resigned.

Pages 16, 17.—Changes in Costa Anglers' Club. Chas. W. Woodhall, president, *vice* Richard Hall, Esq.; hon. sec. and treasurer, Edward Mitchell, Esq., Granville Lodge, Belmont Road, Scarborough. The club water extends from Keld Head to the lower end of Messrs. Tindall's property below Kirkby Misperton Bridge. Limited to thirty subscribing members. Annual subscription now £4 4s., and entrance fee, £5 5s. Grayling season from April 16th to February 28th, and from October 1st to February 28th with any kind of bait below Black Syke. Limit for trout, 11in. Minnow fishing, for trout only, allowed below Black Syke, from June 16th to October 1st.

Pages 17, 75.—There is now no inn at Kirby Misperton.

L

Page 19.—Day tickets issued by the Harrogate Angling Association to visitors are now 5s.

Page 20.—The Harrogate Angling Association are allowed to fish, by permission, the length of the Crimple from Almsford Bridge to Fulford Grange. A special ticket for this water is issued to members only (2s. 6d. each) for one day a week.

Page 25.—The Derwent Anglers' Club 5/- day ticket allows the holder to fish the whole of the club water, except in May or June as stated. April 15th should read 16th.

Page 43.—A new rule of the Esk Fishery Association, the outcome of a recent controversy, is that all salmon, salmon trout, or bull trout foul-hooked must be forthwith returned to the water with as little injury as possible.

Page 54.—The Yorkshire Fishery Board have this season placed 1,000 yearling trout in the River Hull, below the top lock.

Pages 57, 99—106.—The Tees Fishery Board have this season turned a large quantity of young trout into the Tees at Croft, Gainford, Barnard Castle, Middleton-in-Teesdale, and also into the River Leven and Thorpe Beck. A large consignment of salmon fry were turned into the Tees at Wynch Bridge, below High Force, at Middleton-in-Teesdale, and into the Grand Beck at Gainford.

Page 63.—Most of the River Nidd between Ramsgill and Wath Bridge is embraced in the Bradford Corporation Reservoir scheme, now in progress. This will spoil the fishing for a time. The fishing on the north side of the river for about two miles above Wath Bridge and one mile below belongs to Mr. Barlow, of Wath, who occasionally grants leave. Plenty of fish, running about 4 to 1lb. A short rod is necessary on the higher reaches of the Nidd.

Page 64.—The Harrogate Conservative Angling Association are allowed to fish Mr. Bland's water on the Nidd, at Dacre Banks. The club have this season turned a large supply of yearling trout into their length on this river. The Harrogate Angling Association have also turned 6,000 trout fry and 200 two-year-olds into their water at Darley.

Page 65.—The Knaresborough Anglers' Club water now extends on the north side of the Nidd up to Holly Bank Wood. The Knaresborough Joint Angling Clubs have this season turned 2,000 yearling trout into the Nidd at Knaresborough, in addition to 600 yearlings contributed by the Harrogate Angling Association.

Page 67, *line* 22.—Harrogate Conservative Angling Association should read Harrogate Angling Association. For subscriptions, tickets, &c., see page 19.

Page 81.—The Clitheroe Association now hold the water from Higher Horrocksford to Mr. Eli Tucker's, on the Lancashire side, and from Bank Hall right away through to Bradford Bridge, on the Yorkshire side. The club have this season turned 2,000 yearling trout into their water. The 8-inch limit will be strictly enforced. The changes in the club officials are:—president, Wm. King Wilkinson, Esq.; vice-president, A. W. Dewhurst, Esq.; committee, Messrs. A. Sykes, T. Shaw, H. M. Rowland, F. Sykes, J. Allen, J. Lofthouse, and J. Robinson; water bailiff, William Oddie, 13, Church Brow, Clitheroe.

Page 82, *line* 7.—Whalley should read Mitton.

Pages 87, 90.—There is now no inn at Brawby.

Page 90.—A weir has been constructed at Appleton Mill on the Seven, which has improved the fishing.

Page 97.—The inns at Holme, Baldersby, and Skipton-upon-Swale are now done away with.

Page 106.—The Stockton Angling Association have erected a fishing hut for refreshments, &c., on their length of water on the Tees. This association have their own hatcheries. The Fishery Board Hatcheries are at Dinsdale.

Page 111.—The Tanfield Angling Club now grant six-day tickets in place of three, to members, for the use of friends. The entrance fee is raised to £5 5s.

Pages 114, 115.—For Keasden Beck read Grisden Beck. From the third field below Wenning Bridge to Grisden Beck, on the south side of the River Wenning, the fishing belongs to the Manningham Angling Club. President, Mr. J. W. Broadbent; hon. sec., Mr. John Cowen, 29, Salem Street, Bradford, from whom complimentary tickets, 2s. 6d. each, may be had for outsiders when accompanied by a member. This club has also a considerable length of water on Grisden Beck and a mile or more at Newsome Dene Beck, Goose Eye, near Keighley. Limit for trout, 6in.

Page 126.—The Tadcaster Angling and Preservation Society in May last re-stocked their water on the Wharfe with perch and rudd, and in June another consignment of fish were turned into their length. There are a few changes in this club. The president is Chas. J. Ireland, Esq.; *vice*, Wm Smith, Esq.; assistant secretary, Mr. Benj. Carr; water bailiff, James Beaumont; *vice*, W. Walsh, dead. Page 126, bottom line but one, read Thomas Fielding, Esq. for John Fielden, Esq.

Every angler who cherishes good sport combined with a desire to enjoy nature at her loveliest, to see her attired in her beauteous garb of eternal green, to appreciate her ever-varying charms—deep wooded and sweeping uplands, grassy glades and sylvan bowers, dancing streams, and deep pools rippled o'er by soft breezes and and lifting with speckled trout—should sojourn at Grassington in the very heart of Upper Wharfedale. And if the Angler, Sportsman, Tourist, or Health-Seeker would enjoy home comforts, the best accommodation, and reasonable charges, let him take up his abode at Grassington House, where there is everything to make the heart happy and life endurable. Fish preservation and re-stocking have been so ardently indulged in, that the streams in Upper Wharfedale have been brought to a high state of perfection, and there is no better angling centre in Yorkshire than Grassington, whose landscapes and river scenery have a wide reputation. One might say in the words of Sir Walter Scott, not the Wharfe alone "in dawning bright, shall rush upon the ravished sight; but many a tributary stream, each from its own dark dell shall gleam." Thus amidst scenes that are brightest there are tight lines and full panniers coupled with the health-giving comforts of Grassington House.—*Advt.*

COWBROUGHS' STANDARD BLENDS.

OF

SCOTCH WHISKIES.

"E.Y.O." (registered)	"Islay"
"Glenlivet"	"Campbelltown"
"Lochaber"	"Highland Malt"
"Toddy"	"Lowland Malt"

"Special Liqueur."

The conviction long existing in the trade is now steadily growing amongst consumers, that a Blend of Scotch Whiskies, *when selected with the requisite care and judgment,* is superior in every quality to the product of one Distillery, which, in most cases, is too pronounced in its flavour, &c., to be palatable to the majority of consumers.

It is also well known to the Trade that almost every blend made up by Houses in Scotland for the English Market, contains a very large percentage of grain spirit, used for the purpose of cheapening the price, good in itself when old, but much inferior to Whisky distilled from pure malt.

We guarantee all our Scotch Whiskies to be distilled from malt only, and to contain NO GRAIN SPIRIT.

We hold one of the largest Bonded Stocks of high-class Scotch Whisky in the country, and which comprises all the best makes; and we have special facilities—possessed by few firms—for supplying fine old matured Whiskies.

Our Whiskies have been selected and Blended with the greatest care and judgment, each one being composed of the choicest Whiskies made in the different districts, and is the highest type of Whisky procurable in each style.

Single Whiskies may be had by those who prefer them to Blends.

"THE PERFECTION OF SCOTCH WHISKY."

Absolutely Pure and free from all flavouring ingredients.

"E.Y.O." (Registered) (Eight years old.)

A Blend of Whiskies produced at the oldest and most-famed Distilleries in Scotland, **matured in wood by age only.**

This Whisky shows the high perfection obtained by long experience in the selecting and skill in the blending of Scotch Whiskies. Its extreme softness and mellowness, and its fine character, are produced by great age, high quality, and judicious blending. Being entirely free from saccharine, it possesses medicinal properties of exceptional value, and is unquestionably

"The Perfection of Scotch Whisky."

Guaranteed to contain NO GRAIN SPIRIT.

42/- ~~41/-~~ PER DOZEN.

VERY OLD "SPECIAL LIQUEUR" WHISKY.

This Whisky is quite unique in style and character. It is a perfectly balanced blend of the produce of the most famous Highland Distilleries, matured in fine Sherry Wood for very many years in our own Bonded Stores. It possesses, in a remarkable degree, the rich colour, great body, softness, delicacy, and piquant bouquet—the fragrancy of the peat and the heather—so characteristic of, and only to be found in the highest class Highland Malt Whiskies when obtained in their native purity, and unmixed with Grain Spirit.

Guaranteed to contain NO GRAIN SPIRIT

60/- PER DOZEN.

"GLENLIVET." (Seven years old.)

A Blend of the best Whiskies made in the Glenlivet district. It has a special flavour which cannot be imitated and is greatly appreciated by good judges of high-class Whisky. The various Whiskies composing this Blend have been warehoused in our Excise Bonded Stores since the period of distillation, and are now perfectly matured.

Guaranteed to contain NO GRAIN SPIRIT.

46/- ~~45/-~~ PER DOZEN.

"LOCHABER." (Seven years old.)

A Blend of the finest Whiskies distilled in Nether Lochaber and the adjacent Islands on the West Coast of Scotland. It possesses a delicious mellow flavour, and the quality cannot be excelled. Bonded in selected Sherry Casks and now thoroughly matured.

Guaranteed to contain NO GRAIN SPIRIT.

46/- ~~45/-~~ PER DOZEN

"TODDY." (Six years old.)

A Blend of the very cream of Lowland Malt Whiskies, principally distilled in the Midland and Eastern Counties of Scotland; matured in Sherry Wood; has a soft, mellow flavour, and great richness of body, and is specially suited for using with hot water.

Guaranteed to contain NO GRAIN SPIRIT.

42/- ~~41/-~~ PER DOZEN.

"ISLAY." (Six years old.)

A Blend of the choicest Whiskies distilled on the Island. It is stored in oak wood, and has no colour beyond what accrues from age. It possesses a peculiar, peaty soft flavour. This flavour is acquired at an early period of manufacture by drying the malt in a kiln heated by a peat fire. The softness is developed by AGE ONLY.

Guaranteed to contain NO GRAIN SPIRIT.

38/- ~~37/-~~ PER DOZEN.

"CAMPBELLTOWN," (Six years old.)

A Blend of the finest Whiskies made in the West Highlands of Scotland. The various Whiskies have been warehoused in our Excise Bonded Stores since the period of distillation, and are now thoroughly matured. This Blend has a full flavour, but not so pronounced as the "Islay." It is well adapted for using with cold water, as is now so customary.

Guarranteed to contain NO GRAIN SPIRIT.

38/- ~~37/-~~ PER DOZEN.

"HIGHLAND MALT," (Five years old.)

A Blend of the finest Whiskies distilled in the far North of Scotland. Each Whisky is matured at the different distilleries in our own Sherry Casks. It possesses a rich, mellow flavour, and is specially suitable for those who do not like very high-flavoured Whiskies.

Guaranteed to contain NO GRAIN SPIRIT.

38/- ~~37/-~~ PER DOZEN.

"LOWLAND MALT," (Four years old.)

The Whiskies composing this Blend are distilled in the Southern and South-Western Counties of Scotland. It is almost silent-flavoured, the barley being malted in the ordinary way and the Whiskies stored in plain wood. Equal to what is sold by many houses at 37/- per dozen.

Guaranteed to contain NO GRAIN SPIRIT.

34/- ~~33/-~~ PER DOZEN.

Bottles are charged 1/- per dozen extra; and cases to hold one dozen bottles, are charged 1/- each. The full value of the packages is credited when the empties are returned to us in good condition.

Quotations for these Whiskies in Bulk for Home and Export Trade on application.

A single bottle of any of these Whiskies forwarded by parcels post—as sample—on receipt of amount pro rata, with 6d. added to cover part postage and package.

INDEX.

M